Embroidery and lace; their manufacture and history from the remotest antiquity to the present day. A handbook for amateurs, collectors, and general readers

Lefébure, Ernest

BIBLIOLIFE

EMBROIDERY

AND

LACE:

THEIR MANUFACTURE AND HISTORY FROM THE REMOTEST ANTIQUITY TO THE PRESENT DAY.

A HANDBOOK FOR AMATEURS, COLLECTORS, AND GENERAL READERS.

BY

ERNEST LEFÉBURE,

Lace Manufacturer and Administrator of the Musée des Arts Décoratifs, Paris.

TRANSLATED AND ENLARGED, WITH NOTES, BY

ALAN S. COLE,

Author of "Ancient Needlepoint and Pillow Lace," Descriptive Catalogues of the Lace, Tapestry, and Embroidery Collections in South Kensington Museum, etc.

WITH ONE HUNDRED AND FIFTY-SIX WOODCUTS.

LONDON:

H. GREVEL AND CO.,

33, KING STREET, COVENT GARDEN, W.C.

1888.

PREFACE.

THIS book has been compiled with the view of supplying a link which has been missing in the history of embroidery, no serious work on this fascinating subject having been hitherto published. This may appear strange when one reflects that few arts have been more universally practised. True, several books have been written about various classes and aspects of embroidery. Amongst others, there are Lady Marian Alford's *Needlework as Art*, Miss Dolby's *Church Embroidery*, Miss Higgins' *Handbook of Embroidery*, Dr. Rock's *Textile Fabrics*, and the Countess of Wilton's *Art of Needlework*. Some of these are rather out of date; none can be held to fulfil the same purpose as Monsieur Lefébure's book in dealing with the technical character of embroidery, and in presenting a succinct and comprehensive sketch of its history, to instruct needlewomen and to serve as a guide to amateurs interested in the subject.

Lace-making is more fortunate than embroidery in having been historically discussed by many authors, to whom we are indebted for the principal facts which appear in the chapters devoted to this industry ; their names are so frequently cited in the course of our remarks, that it seems unnecessary to mention them here. We are none the less indebted to them for assistance in the second part of this work.

We have adopted the classification of needlepoint laces, and those made on the pillow with bobbins ; a classification which is of primary importance, and has not been effectually established by writers who have preceded us. This will help readers to detect different makes of laces most diverse in appearance, and it will guard them from confusing one class with the other. Lace is the most poetic of all textile tissues, and has been sung in verse. So far from veiling beauty, it surrounds it with a filmy aureole or environment of such appropriateness as to have inspired many poets. The historian's duty, however, is to take account of precise facts; we have therefore borrowed but little from the legends and verses concerning lace-making.

Our aim, moreover, is not only to give instruction by a record of facts, but, above all, to centre interest upon the *rôle* which woman's labour plays in the artistic productions of the world. And the temptation presents itself of inquiring whether it is not rather by the needle and the bobbin than by the brush, the graver, or the chisel, etc., that the influence of woman should assert itself in the arts. She is sovereign in the domain of art needle-work; few men would care to dispute with her the right of using those delicate implements, so intimately associated with the dexterity of her nimble and slender fingers. But do intelligent women sufficiently encourage the results of this association? Could they not give more attention, study, and effort, to stimulate a fuller development of artistic work produced by the needle and the bobbin?

To bring such questions home to impressionable natures of generous aspirations, is, we hope, to instigate in many directions a progress of knowledge and opinion through which it may be recognized that the productions of embroidery and lace-making are worthy of standing upon the same level with those of painting, engraving, and sculpture, and of being represented in our public museums.

The satisfaction that we have rendered some service in writing the following pages, will confer upon us the best recompense for a work to which we have striven to bring all our ability, coupled with the affection in which we hold our industry.

We should mention that this translation contains a number of additional notes, and modifications of certain statements. This is the case, for instance, in respect of Egyptian work referred to on p. 24, and of Greek embroidery (p. 46), where a new illustration is given. Again, the description of Irish laces has been enlarged, and six new engravings have been inserted (pp. 249—254).

TABLE OF CONTENTS.

PILLOW OR BOBBIN LACFS.

EMBROIDERY AND LACE.

PART I.—EMBROIDERY.

CHAPTER I.

DEFINITIONS.

Distinction between an Embroidery and a Lace — Embroidery — Needlepoint Lace—Pillow-made or Bobbin Lace.

THE distinction between embroidery and lace as well as that between embroidery and other ornamental textiles is not popularly appreciated. At the outset therefore of a work like the present, intended for those who wish to study such matters, it will be well to describe briefly the distinctive features of the different methods or processes by which ornamental tissues are produced.

Definitions.—There are three methods or processes for producing ornamental tissues :—

(1) By hand-painting or printing in colours ; (2) By weaving ; (3) By needlework (embroidery).

1. Hand-painting in colours to decorate a textile is

I

employed particularly for fans, and for certain imitations of tapestry hangings. Printing in colours by means of engraved blocks or cylinders is, however, more common. These processes, while lacking neither charm nor brightness in their effects, are nevertheless distinctively of a superficial character.

2. Weaving consists in so disposing the threads with which an ornamental textile is to be made, that certain selected ones are, from time to time, visible on its surface, and effects of pattern and colour are thus obtained, possessing more substantial definition than results from either painting or printing.

Methods of ornamental weaving have been known from the earliest times, and may be broadly classed under two sections : firstly, figured loom-weaving, which was brought to so high a perfection by Jacquard's invention of his apparatus at the commencement of this century; secondly, tapestry-weaving in high and low warp frames, in the manners to be seen respectively at the Gobelins and Beauvais factories.

3. Lastly, the third method of ornamenting a textile is that with which we are specially to concern ourselves in the first part of our book, namely ornamental needle-work, or embroidery.

Embroidery.—Embroidery sometimes allies itself with the two first named processes in accentuating, by means either of stitches wrought over, or by skilfully outlining, certain portions of the pattern in a printed or woven textile to which it is desired to

* See *A Short History of Tapestry*, by Eugène Müntz (Cassell & Co., Limited).

give prominence. But embroidery is more frequently used by itself for decorating a plain stuff; and since the practice of this handicraft is freer and more independent than that of printing or weaving, it is capable of more easily producing really artistic effects.

The Needle.— The embroiderer's worktool is the needle, which may be regarded as little more than a stiff and pointed continuation of the flexible thread. Primitively the needle was a thorn or fishbone; subsequently it was made in wood, bone, and ivory before it assumed shape in metal.

Fig. 1.—A lady embroidering (after Abraham Bosse).

In the hands of an able worker it is one of the most precious implements that may be used in the service of art.

Unfettered by any scientific contrivances, which fix limits to the possibilities of a machine, the needle, moving according to the caprice and ingenuity of the fingers guiding it, sweeps with perfect freedom along the surface or through the thickness of a stuff. Like pen or pencil, it can be made to trace forms of any complexity, and, in two words, it writes and draws. Used with a variety of coloured threads, its function resembles that of a brush in depicting tones and shades. Indeed, in a sense, a superiority to the brush may be claimed for it, since it can be made to produce work in relief, an element in decoration which can be successfully resorted to and preserved from abuse, and is certainly outside the powers of painting.

The Crochet Needle.—But besides pointed straightness, the needle has other forms, of which note must be taken in a discussion upon embroidery. At times the needle's point has been converted into a hook, with its opposite and lower extremity sufficiently sharpened to easily pierce a stuff. Thus changed in form, the needle is called a crochet needle, with which a chain stitch is usually worked. The thread, caught by the hook, is carried through the stuff and brought back looped. Thus a peculiar class of stitch frequently employed in embroidery is the result. A distinguishing feature of the crochet as compared with other needles is the absence of a threading eye.

The appliances for doing embroidery are obviously of little bulk, and can be so conveniently carried that a work-woman can put them into her pocket, handy for use on a journey or in her spare moments. The stuff to be embroidered is held in the left hand, whilst the needle is plied with the right (fig. 1).

Frames for Embroidery.—But if the stuff to be embroidered is too large to be carried in the hand,

Fig. 2.—Engraving taken from *L'Encyclopédie* : The art of the embroiderer, by St. Aubin.

or if the embroidery to be done upon it is of such a nature that both hands must be engaged in working the needle, different sorts of frames, in which the stuff can be tautly stretched, become necessary. For big pieces, an adjustable frame with movable battens, resting upon trestles, as shown in fig. 2, is required. Embroidery frames of smaller dimensions consist of parallel bars, kept apart by long wooden screws. These can be twisted to increase or diminish the distance between the two bars, upon which the two opposite sides of the stuff have been first fixed, and so adjust the frame to the size of the stuff, stretching it out firmly (fig. 3). Other frames, again, especially those for crochet embroidery, are similar to the circular band of a sieve. It is said that we are indebted to China for this class of frame. Upon it the stuff to be embroidered is stretched like the sheepskin of a drum, whence the expression *tambour* embroidery. In the last century this was fancifully termed *broderie au boisseau* (bushel embroidery) (figs. 4 and 5).

Designing for Embroidery.—The employment of skill in using embroidery materials is governed, from the artistic point of view, by the design which may have been selected, and by its careful transfer on to the stuff upon which it is to be wrought. It is evident that mere needlework, however dexterous, cannot redeem bad taste in design. To weigh well the nature and character of the object to be decorated, to employ suitable threads, colours and materials which shall harmonize with the foundation on which the intended embroidery is to be produced, to follow sound principles in composing the pattern without thereby fettering artistic initiative, are rules as eternally true in respect of embroidery as in other arts. Unfortunately much embroidery, often perfect in its needlework, errs in quality of design and in the use of colours and tones which create discordant effects when brought into close juxtaposition. A suitable design having been chosen, its transfer on to material has then to be managed in such a way that the

Fig. 3.—Mademoiselle Dugrenot's embroidery frame.

designer's intention may be faithfully carried out by the skilful needle-worker. Methods of transferring designs are various; the best is for the designer himself to draw the pattern with pencil or chalk upon the material; for important pieces this is an operation not to be delegated to any other hand. In less important cases, the lines of the designer's drawing upon paper may be pricked with needle

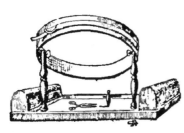

Fig. 4.—Tambour embroidery frame (St. Aubin).

holes, through which coloured resinous powder can be rubbed or shaken on to the stuff beneath; to this when warmed the powdered reproduction of the pattern adheres. Books on ladies' fancy work generally contain descriptions of methods more or less ingenious for effecting pattern transfers. When canvas or textile fabrics with equally distinct reticulations are to be embroidered, the transfer of a pattern can be managed if the designer carefully marks his pattern with reticulations numbered to correspond with those of the material; in this case the work is called *à points comptés* (stitching by counting).

One or other of the foregoing methods of transferring the pattern and fixing the stuff in a frame having been carried out, the work of embroidery then commences.

Fig. 5.—Tambour embroidery frame (St. Aubin).

Methods of Working.—To embroider the material mounted in a rectangular or circular frame, the needle-worker places one hand beneath, and the other above, the stuff, and makes the stitches by passing the needle through it from one hand to the other.

This operation is to be noted, for to some extent stitches in a sewing machine are made similarly. The machines specially adapted to embroider are fitted with ingenious contrivances, whereby such an operation is simulated. But we shall return to this point further on, when discussing modern embroideries.

Now, whether the stuff being embroidered be held in the hand or the frame, the fact is patent that embroidery is an ornamental needlework done upon a stuff of some sort. Embroidery postulates a material foundation. And the character of this foundation has to be duly appreciated in the course of scheming a design which shall be appropriately worked on to it. Notwithstanding that certain classes of embroidery are worked in such a way as to cover and conceal the ground, as, for instance, when canvas or other plain textiles are used, the margin which may ultimately be placed about such embroideries exacts a harmony between it and them. So that even these embroideries are not exempt from the fulfilment of those general conditions already laid down, neither are they examples of departure from the definition that embroidery is an ornamental needlework wrought upon a texture of some sort.

These remarks have been necessary in order that the distinguishing difference between embroidery and lace may be well established. We therefore proceed to describe lace.

Lace.—First let us clearly state that lace-making is not a process involving the use of some already existing fabric. Lace itself is a textile fabric, of which both ground and pattern are entirely produced by the lace-maker. It is a member of the same family as knitted and netted work and twisted and knotted thread trimmings (*passementerie*). Lace-making is of two distinctly different methods. One method calls the needle into operation, the other a series of bobbins. Hence the two marked categories, needlepoint lace and bobbin, or, as it is usually called, pillow lace.

Needlepoint lace is made by first stitching thread along the outlines of a pattern drawn or transferred upon paper or parchment, by which means a skeleton thread pattern is produced (see the outline sprigs and spray in fig. 6). This skeleton thread work serves as the scaffolding, as one might call it, upon and between which the stitches, for the shapes and ground connecting them together, are cast, and so wrought into needlepoint lace. Whilst the taking of these stitches bears close

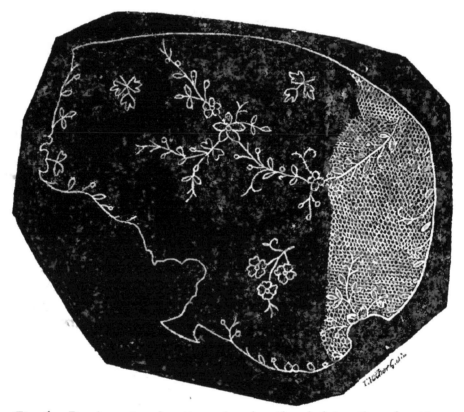

Fig. 6.—Parchment and pattern showing the skeleton thread pattern and needlepoint lace in progress.

analogy to those in embroidery, it will have been perceived that the work thus produced is altogether different from embroidery, since it has started from no previously provided textile fabric.

Design for a Needlepoint Lace.—A design for a needlepoint lace should evince the designer's sense of this last-mentioned characteristic; and it naturally follows that the same pattern cannot be indiscriminately employed for an embroidery and a lace. The designer of a pattern to be embroidered is compelled to consider his textile as the foundation from which he starts, whereas the designer for lace has first to acquaint himself with the dimensions of the proposed work. To aim at harmonious unity,

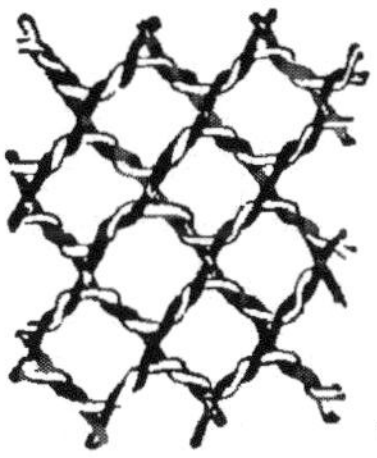

Fig. 7.—Specimen of a pillow lace ground of meshes.

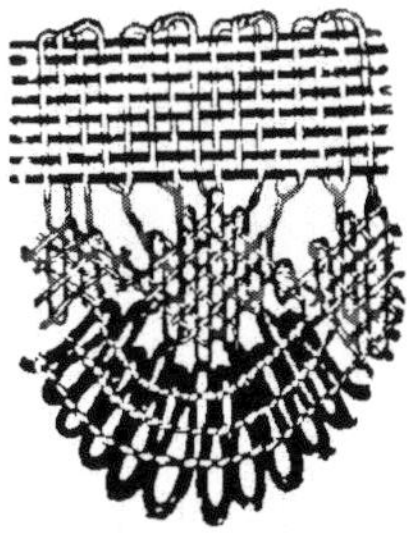

Fig. 8.—Specimen of close and open thread work in pillow lace.

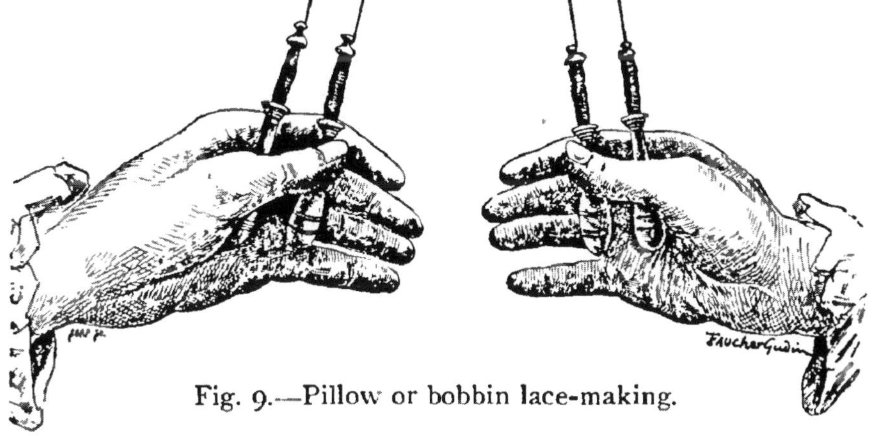

Fig. 9.—Pillow or bobbin lace-making.

balance of, and contrast between, the open and close portions of the filmy fabric, graceful and continuous curves or indentations along the borders, and to infuse an influence of lace-like lightness and suppleness into his pattern, are briefly and broadly stated principles which should guide a designer for lace.

Method of Work.—The preparations for making lace with the needle are extremely simple. The pattern, having been decided upon, is carefully drawn with ink in fine, firm outline upon pieces of stiff paper, fine oil-cloth, parchment, or vellum. Each such piece containing a portion of the pattern should be of a size to be easily handled by the lace-worker, and special care must be taken that the boundary lines of these separate portions of the pattern may follow edges of blossoms, stems, or ornamental shapes, in order that when the various portions are joined together the junctures between them shall be invisible in the completed lace. Holes pricked along the lines of the pattern help the lace-maker in accurately laying threads and stitching them down upon the lines. The paper or parchment pattern has then to be backed with a piece of linen or similar material, which answers two purposes: the one to prevent the pattern from being torn during the construction upon its surface of the thread skeleton pattern ; the second to facilitate the detachment of the completed lace from its pattern, by simply cutting, between the paper and the linen, the threads stitched through both at the time the thread skeleton pattern was fastened on to the surface of the paper or parchment (fig. 6). As soon as the several portions into which the whole pattern has been cut are finished, they are detached from their respective papers or parchments, brought together, and united by needle stitches, the junctures being as effectually concealed as possible. The piece of needlepoint lace is thus completed.

Bobbin or Pillow Lace.—The make of a bobbin or pillow lace has considerably less analogy with an embroidery than that existing between this latter and a needlepoint lace. Bobbin or pillow lace-making more nearly resembles weaving. The threads for making a bobbin or pillow lace are fixed upon a circular or square ushion or pillow, placed variously to suit the methods

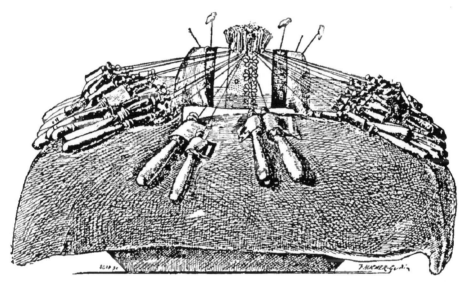

Fig. 10.—Cushion and bobbins for pillow lace-making.

of manufacture in vogue in different countries. One end of each thread is fastened on to the cushion with a pin, the main supply of thread being twined round a small bobbin of wood, bone or ivory. The threads are twisted and plaited together by the lace-maker's throwing her bobbins over and under one another. This operation is fairly simple, since children of eight or nine years of age can be successfully trained to it. It nevertheless demands considerable dexterity with the fingers. However numerous the bobbins may be, they are generally worked by groups of four (see fig. 7). By crossing, plaiting, and twisting her threads the lace-maker forms the close and open parts of the work, which grows into the fabric known as pillow lace (see fig. 8).

Design for Bobbin or Pillow Lace.—The design for bobbin or pillow lace must of course be adapted to the technical requirements of the process, and cannot therefore be the same as one for needlepoint lace. Needlepoint lace undoubtedly has an appearance of greater strength and nobility than pillow lace, and for this reason it was in former times generally preferred for occasions of state by wearers who had reached a certain time of life. On the other hand, bobbin or pillow lace has the quality of charming suppleness; and for use in mantillas, veils, and *fichus* it is better than needlepoint lace, lending itself with delicate softness and graceful flexibility as a covering to the head and shoulders of a woman. Designs then for such a fabric should reflect their author's perception of these subtle qualities—a statement confirming the truism in regard to decorative arts that a sense of the peculiar and most appropriate employment of any art furnishes a key-note to the artist who conscientiously seeks to inform his compositions with a perfect harmony.

Method of Working.—In twisting and plaiting the threads, the lace-maker requires certain fixed points in the pattern, by which she may avoid entanglements (see figs. 10 and 11). This she secures by sticking pins into the pattern over which she is working upon the completion of each open stitch. The precise position for the pinholes must be carefully determined and indicated upon the pattern before the lace is begun. The cutting up of a pillow lace pattern into convenient portions differs in some cases from the corresponding operation for needlepoint laces. Excepting in certain styles of Flemish pillow lace, where the separation of the pattern into portions is similar to that for needlepoint lace, the majority of pillow lace patterns can be cut into strips or bands, the laces made from which are subsequently united together by a stitch called the *point de racroc.*

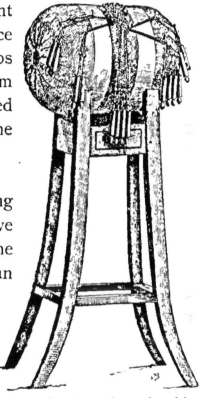

Point de Racroc (uniting stitch).—This is said to have been invented at Bayeux in the last century by a workwoman named Cahanet. It opened the way to the manufacture of pieces of pillow lace much larger than those made before its invention. It consists in finishing off the two outer parallel edges of a strip of pillow

Fig. 11.—Another class of cushion and its support for pillow lace-making (taken from the *Traité de la Dentelle*, by Louise d'Alq).

lace with a series of half, instead of whole, meshes. To unite two separate strips it is necessary to bring the edge of one close to the edge of the other, and then with a needle to complete the intermediate meshes. By this means, when very carefully done, several strips are joined to one another in a way that defies detection even when the junctures occur in simple meshed grounds.

Summary.—It will have been seen from the foregoing that embroidery is perfectly distinct from lace-making, and that needlepoint and pillow laces are produced by such totally different methods as to prevent their being confused one with the other.

Being thus clearly enlightened and protected from future errors in distinguishing embroidery from lace, we will merely add that embroidery certainly preceded the invention of lace. Later on we shall see that it is very doubtful if the making of lace, properly so called, was known to the ancients, although it is absolutely proved that embroidery has been practised from the earliest of times. Accordingly we will now deal with the history of embroidery, after which we shall turn our attention to laces.

CHAPTER II.

THE EMBROIDERY OF ANTIQUITY.

Threads.—The needle was obviously invented in the first place for simply sewing stuffs together; it was soon afterwards put to the more intricate work of ornamenting them. Thus arose the art of embroidery. Threads similar to such as were primarily spun for weaving purposes were pressed into the service of the newly found art. Those of weak tension were twisted together to form single threads of the necessary strength. In this way threads of different dimensions were spun, and the embroiderers were furnished with a means of giving a variety of effects to their work.

Successive discoveries in connection with dyeing processes provided embroiderers, in a corresponding manner, with a complete scale or series of colours. The earlier threads were of wool, flax, and cotton. Of later date were silken threads.

Wool.—From flocks of goats and sheep such as were tended by shepherd patriarchs, men derived meat for sustenance and wools for clothing. It is fair to assume perhaps that primeval threads were of wool.

But we must not here forget that, in the early centuries of antiquity, Egypt, mistress of an advanced civilization which was conspicuous for its highly

2

developed industries, was noted, as it is nowadays, for plants like hemp and flax, the fibrous bark of which yielded filaments for the manufacture of thread, etc. From hemp, strands of ropes and strings of fishing nets were made.

Flax.—Tradition assigns the invention of flax to Isis. It is used for weaving the compact and pliant textile called linen, and bleaches rapidly. Linen was held to be the particular textile suited to religious usages, and became the emblem of purity. Sacrificial priests were robed in it; altar, ceremonial, and funeral cloths were made of it; and their borders were embroidered to mark the sacred services to which they were appropriated. According to the precepts contained in Exodus chap. xxxi., the vestments of the high-priest Aaron and his sons were of linen. The ephod of the high-priest was a sort of linen vest, ornamented with colours of the jacinth, and in purple and crimson; upon the pectoral, or breastplate, twelve precious stones were set, bearing the names of the twelve sons of Jacob.*

Cotton.—During this period, too, cotton, which naturally grows there, was used in India, whence, from the banks of the Ganges and the Indus, merchants' caravans conveyed it to the peoples of Northern Asia and of Egypt. But the Greeks seem to have remained unacquainted with it until B.C. 333, when, in the course of their conquering progress under Alexander the Great, they noticed (according to Strabo)† that the clothes of their vanquished opponents were made of " tree wool,"

---

* *History of the People of Israel,* by Ledrain, t. i., p. 140.
† Strabo, Book XV., chap. i.

or of "wool growing out of nuts," both of which descriptions, however scientifically deficient, clearly apply to cotton.

Silk.—As to silk, although it has the reputation of having been known to the Chinese B.C. 1200, and of being styled by them the "Divine thread," it was virtually a new and rare material in the West at the time of Julius Cæsar. Aristotle, some four hundred years earlier, mentions the Βόμβυξ as a large worm, subject to three metamorphoses,* and says that, in the Isle of Cos, Pamphile, daughter of Plates, unwound the first silk cocoon there, and with the fibre wove a tissue. But such references are isolated. Persia, India, and perhaps Egypt began to weave with silk not sooner than a few years before Christ; and it was from these countries that Rome first began to import silks about the time of Julius Cæsar. Virgil, in his Second Georgic, is one of the first of the Roman authors to write about silk. During the reign of the Emperor Tiberius the price of silk was enormous; it was worth its weight in gold. "*Libra enim auri libra serici fuit*"—a pound of gold for a pound of silk.

Gold Threads.—But long anterior to the employment of silk in embroideries they had been rendered sumptuous with gold and silver threads.

The idea of beating out gold and silver into thin leaves or sheets, cutting them up into little ribbons, and intermixing them with threads for weaving purposes, is to be traced back almost to the first of historic periods.

* Aristotle, *Ancient History*, Book XIX.

Pliny attributes its conception to Attalus, King of
Asia.* He writes that, in Asia, Attalus discovered a
method of using gold threads in embroidery, and that
the stuffs so embellished were termed Attalic. David†
in his Psalms sings the glories of the golden apparel
in which the king's daughter was arrayed; whilst
Dionysius of Halicarnassus assures us that Tarquinius
Priscus was the first to appear in Rome wearing a gold-
embroidered robe.

These various references surely establish the fact
that from the very commencement of the art the
needle, together with threads of different sizes,
colours, and values, has been the embroiderer's
indispensable implement, the essential characteristic
of which has scarcely altered during the lapse of
many centuries.

Proofs of the Antiquity of Embroidery.—As the investigation of our subject is made more and more
searching, so abundant proofs are brought to light that
embroidery is one of the most ancient of the arts.
The want of badges or emblems to mark social
distinctions led to the ornamentation of garments as
soon almost as they came into use. The simple and
ready execution of embroidery, which, as we have
shown, required but a needle and thread, yielded
obvious means for gratifying a craving for marks
distinctive of a chief's costume, for the enrichment
of accessories to religious rituals, or for the satisfaction of that innate desire on the part of women to
please by ingeniously adorning their natural beauty.

---

* Pliny, *Natural History*, Book VIII.
† Holy Bible, Psalm xliv.

Savage Tribes.—Certain usages amongst primitive tribes of Africa give grounds for the theory that, under certain conditions, the practice of embroidery may actually have preceded that of weaving. An instance in point is cited concerning negro girls, whose costume consisted of either a necklace or belt of feathers. When of

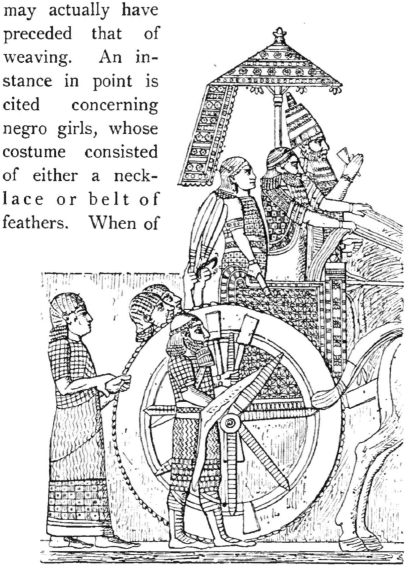

Fig. 12.—King Assurnazirpal (from the Nimroud alabaster bas-relief).

a marriageable age, these girls embroidered their skins with figures of flowers and animals in vivid colours.

The Assyrians.—Without stretch of imagination, we

are led to the conclusion that much of the ornament
upon the costumes of figures represented in very
early Assyrian monuments was of embroidery. The
Nimroud bas-reliefs sculptured in alabaster are mentioned by Messrs. Perrot and Chipiez, who direct
attention to the embroidered vestments of King
Assurnazirpal thereon depicted (fig. 12).

The Jews.—The Bible is replete with descriptions
of embroideries, frequently referring with minuteness
to their details. But, above all, it surprises one to
find that embroiderers at those remote times had
brought their art to so high a standard of execution
as to be able to render the most elaborate of subjects.
In Exodus, for instance, we read how Moses caused
a veil or curtain of fine twined linen to be cunningly
embroidered with cherubim of blue and purple and
scarlet, for the holy of holies. It was bordered
with loops, and made fast by fifty gold rings to gilt-
wood pillars.

Solomon, whose splendours are proverbial, ordered
a curtain to be made for the Temple of azure-coloured
material, upon which purple and scarlet cherubim
were embroidered. On other hangings he directed
that all sorts of flowers and fruits of the earth should
be embroidered. Everything, in fact, suited to ornamental treatment, excepting representations of animal
life, was used.

Ezekiel in his lamentation for Tyrus—"situate at
the entry of the sea, which art a merchant of the
people for many isles "—exclaims, "The merchants
of Sheba, Asshur, and Chilmad were thy merchants.
These were thy merchants in all sorts of things, in

blue clothes and broidered works, and in chests of rich apparel," etc.   Another part of the same chapter (xxvii.) speaks of the "fine linen with broidered work from Egypt," which "was that which thou spreadest forth to be thy sail"* (see fig. 13).

Finally, Josephus, in his *Wars of the Jews*, relates that the veil presented by Herod (B.C. 19) to the

Fig. 13.—Egyptian sailing boat (Gardner Wilkinson's *Ancient Egyptians*, vol. ii., p. 167).

Temple was a Babylonian curtain, fifty cubits high, sixteen broad, embroidered in blue and red, and of marvellous texture.   In a variety of colours the universe, the stars, and elements were represented.

These few, of numerous similar references, prove that with the Jews the art of embroidery reached to a great pitch of perfection during those now distant epochs.

* Holy Bible, Ezek. xxvii.

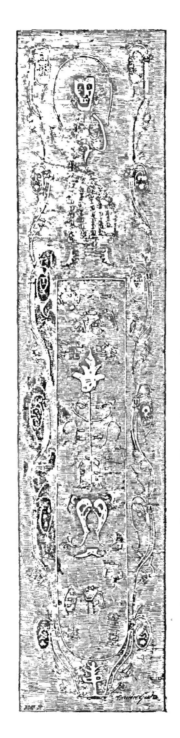

Fig. 14.—Band from an Egyptian shroud in the Musée des Arts Décoratifs.

The Egyptians. — But it should be observed that the Egyptians cultivated the art of embroidery earlier than the Jews. These latter, indeed, were initiated into the craft by the former.* Upon mummy cloths dating from the first of historic periods, plain stitching was used as a rule; but we have also examples of the embroideries then in vogue, of which we are glad to be able to give an illustration (fig. 14). Venerable relics of antiquity, except for the extraordinary

Fig. 15.

care with which the piety of the Egyptians has preserved you, you would have crumbled into dust, like other tissues made during the first ten thousand years of human life on this world ! †

     * *Egyptian Archæology*, by Maspero (English translation published by H. Grevel).

† The specimen engraved in fig. 14 is part of a band, or *clavus*,

Many of the paintings upon Egyptian wooden sar-
cophagi clearly reveal the embroideries of clothing
worn by important personages (fig. 15). The walls
of the Necropolis at Thebes, with their painted
portraits of Rameses III. (fig. 16), of Pharaoh
Mienptah-Hotephimak, and of Queen Taia (fig. 17),
consort of Amenhophis III.,* convey undeniable proofs
that the robes of such sovereigns, at least, were embroidered.

The Greeks.—The Greeks attributed to Minerva
great skill in weaving and needlework. The story of
Arachne, who was changed into a spider for having
dared to compete with the goddess, as told in all its
details by Ovid in the *Metamorphoses*, has been quoted
by all writers upon ancient woven fabrics.

worked with coloured worsteds and flax, in the tapestry-weaving
method, into a tunic rather than a band from a burial cloth. A
considerable number of such specimens have been exhumed from
burial-places along the banks of the Nile, especially from Akhmîm,
in Upper Egypt. It was clearly the custom to bury the dead robed
in ornamented tunics. A very considerable collection of such ornamental textiles is preserved in the Boulak Museum. Both the
British Museum and the South Kensington Museum contain collections of them. For particulars of those at South Kensington
see the recently issued *Descriptive Catalogue of Tapestry and Embroidery* (1888), pp. 1—86. The specimen fig. 14 is presumably
of Christian Coptic work, and dates from the sixth century. At
the same time, it seems not unlikely that work of similar technical
character was produced during the Ptolemaic period in Egypt, and
that the famous corslets described by Herodotus, Book II., chap. clxxxii.,
and Book II., chap. xlvii., were of such a character. In corroboration
of this suggestion, we have specimens of Greek workmanship of the
fourth century before Christ from Kouban (see note on p. 47), in
which bands of leaf ornament and a cloth powdered with ducks are
worked in what may be called the tapestry-weaving (Gobelins)
process.

* See the work by Prisse d'Avennes.

Homer says that Paris brought clever Sidonian embroideresses to Troy. Tyre and Sidon were then at the height of their reputation for ornamental textiles. Again, in the third canto of the *Iliad*, we have a picture of Helen "in her palace embroidering a large cloth, white as alabaster, with the story of the combats in which Trojans skilled in taming steeds and Greeks clad in brazen cuirasses contended for love of her." Then Andromache (canto xxii.) "lines a resplendent robe with a tissue which she embellishes with embroidery of many colours."*

In the *Odyssey* Homer shows us

Fig. 16.—Rameses (Necropolis of Thebes)

* Homer's *Iliad*, cantos xix. and xxii.

"Divine Ulysses wearing an ample purple mantle of fine, soft linen, fastened by a brilliant clasp of gold. The front of the mantle was decorated with rich embroidery, representing a bloodhound who fiercely pins a dappled fawn and casts hungry looks upon the quivering quarry. The spectators were filled with admiration for these marvellous garments, the women fixing their gaze upon the animals wrought in gold, and to all appearance instinct with life."

Fig. 17.—Queen Taia (Necropolis of Thebes).

Fights and scenes of the chase have for many centuries been favourite subjects with embroiderers, and in Homeric times seem to have been rendered with great dexterity. Indians especially never tire of using their needles to depict "animal hunts." *

A description in the *Orestes* of Æschylus is given of how Agamemnon, on his return from Troy, recoiled from placing his feet upon the rich stuffs laid in his way by Clytemnestra. He exclaims, "A mortal to walk upon purple richly embroidered and tissues purchased at great price! No; I dare not do so!"

* *Voyage of Marco Polo to the Indies*, written in 1328.

According to Virgil's *Æneid*, the son of Anchises gave valorous Cleanthes, victor in a fight, a splendid robe described as "a chlamys of golden web, bordered with double meanders in purple. Upon the web was embroidered the son of Tros in a forest, javelin in hand, chasing a fleet hart. He burns with ardour and pants for breath, when suddenly Jove's bird, swooping from the summit of Mount Ida, seizes him in its claws and bears him away to the heavens."

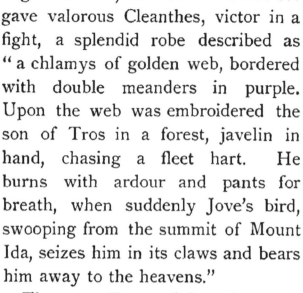

Fig. 18.—Egyptian bronze statue in the museum at Athens.

The spreading and luxurious use of embroideries did not escape the protests of the moralists in ancient times. Diodorus Siculus records that Zaleucus, a Locrian legislator, would only sanction the wearing of embroideries by courtesans. The prophet Ezekiel reproached women with overburdening their dresses with embroidery.

The Babylonians.—Still the riches of Persia, India, Egypt, Chaldæa, Assyria, Babylon, and Phœnicia diffused themselves more and more. Babylon particularly was a centre for the production of most sumptuous embroideries. We have noticed that the veil of the Temple was a Babylonian curtain (πέπλος Βαβυλώνιος), an expression which constantly appears in the writings of ancient authors.

Aristobulus, when describing the tomb of Cyrus, speaks of the great king's body in a golden coffin, which was placed upon a bed of gold curiously wrought, the coverlet whereof was of magnificent Babylonian fabric, gorgeously embroidered.

At Athens the statue of Pallas Athenæ, sculptured by Phidias for the Parthenon, stood in front of an embroidered drapery, hung between the columns at the back.* Every four years it was renewed, and at the Panathenaic festival the peplos of the goddess was carried in procession. This peplos consisted of a large square of crocus-coloured worsted, upon which embroideries were done by Arrephorian virgins,† representing the works of the goddess‡ (fig. 23).

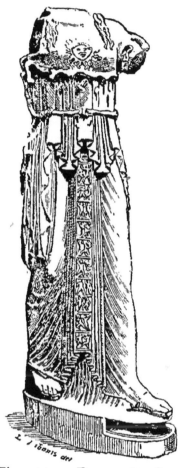

Fig. 19. — Fragment of a Greek statue with embroideries on the drapery.

* See M. de Ronchaud's remarks on the Peplos of Minerva, and his book on *Tapisserie dans l'Antiquité*.

† According to some, the *Arrephori* were four girls of between seven and eleven years of age, two of whom superintended the weaving of the sacred peplos of Athenè. Other authorities say that there is no evidence that the *Arrephori* took part in the Panathenaic festival (see p. 71 of the *British Museum Guide to the Sculptures of the Parthenon*), and it is more generally supposed that the peplos was embroidered by skilful and high-born Athenian ladies.

‡ It should be noted, moreover, that the sacred peplos, borne on

Our museums contain many sculptures and Greek and Etruscan vases on which are figured persons wearing embroideries (see figs. 19, 20, 22, and 23).

A fine stone at the British Museum is engraved with a Babylonian king, Merodach-Idin-Akhy, in embroidered robes, which speak of the art as practised eleven hundred years before Christ (fig. 21).

Fig. 20.—Painting on a Greek vase.

the mast of a ship rolled on wheels in the Panathenaic festival, was destined for the sacred wooden idol, Athenè Polias, which stood in the Erectheus. This peplos "was a woven mantle renewed every five years. On the ground, which is described as dark violet, and also as saffron-coloured, was inwoven the battle of the gods and the giants " (see p. 47 of *British Museum Guide to the Sculptures of the Parthenon*). The central pendent orphrey of the peplos in fig. 19 displays a series of panels containing such subjects. The inweaving of such ornament was possibly, if not probably, done in a method similar to that of Gobelins tapestry-weaving, a method which is distinctly shown in some of the Greek ornamental textiles of the fourth century, discovered in the Tomb of the Seven Brothers, near Temriouk, in the province of Koudan (see *Compte Rendu de la Commission Imperiale Archéologique*, 1878—1879; see also p. 25 *ante*).

Strabo,* in his account of Alexander's campaigns against the Persians, tells us of the astonishment displayed by the Greeks at Megasthenes upon seeing costumes embroidered with gold and jewels, as well as garments of fine gauzy material, like muslin, embroidered with flowers.

From the point of view of their subsequent effect upon industries, these Grecian expeditions of old time into Asia must certainly be held to correspond with the Crusades of much later date. Through contact with Eastern nations, those of the West acquired a taste for articles of beauty and a perception of the manufacturing processes employed in producing them. But a cloudless, sunny sky and a fertile soil remarkable for fauna and flora of incomparable brilliancy in colouring must have been primary sources of inspiration to the Asiatic peoples in respect of the rich and beautiful effects they imparted to their embroideries.

Fig. 21. — Merodach-Idin-Akhy (from an engraved stone in the British Museum).

In the course of his successes, Alexander gained possession of the famous and richly ornamented tent of Darius, an object which excited the admiration and wonder of its captor, who soon afterwards set skilful Cypriotes to work in making for him a magnificent mantle or cloak.

* Strabo, Book XV., chap. i.

Delicate Textiles, Gauze and Muslin.*—The development of appreciation for the charm and glitter of certain classes of embroidery was accompanied with a cultivation of talent to produce equally beautiful articles for other and new purposes;

and Strabo, from whose writings we have already quoted, speaks of the impression made upon the Greeks under Alexander by the sight of golden and jewelled robes, as well as by that of filmy muslin costumes delicately embroidered with floral devices, from which it may be gathered that an equal standard of performance ruled in the dexterous ornamentation of fabrics of aerial lightness, as in the more substantial decoration wrought upon heavier woven materials.

Fig. 22.—Hera, goddess of matrimony (from a Greek vase).

India was, as she remains, long celebrated for the manufacture of transparent muslins, known by poetic appellations, such as *abrawan* (running water), *bafthowa* (woven air), *shubanam* (evening dew), and other similarly expressive

* The names "gauze" and "muslin" are said to be derived from those of the towns Gaza and Mosul.

names.* During the times of which we have been writing, a vast commerce in elegant luxuries, like these gauzy textiles, had evidently been pursued. Ancient sculptures represent dancers draped in tissues of this character, the folds and embroideries of which are so subtly indicated in the sculptures by very light touches that at first sight one concludes that the figures represented are almost absolutely nude. Lucan mentions these gauzes in his descriptions of the festivals provided by Cleopatra at her Alexandrine palace in honour of Cæsar, and particularly of his rival Antony. † Light gauzes were also used for veils. With Oriental gauzes opulent dames of Rome wreathed their heads upon going to the temple, and named such

Fig. 23.—Pallas Athenæ (from a Greek vase in the Louvre).

drapery *flammeum*. The *flammeum* was even used by

* Sir George Birdwood's *The Industrial Arts of India*, vol. ii., p. 93.
† Lucan, Book X.

early Christians, for one of their first authors, in the reign of Tiberius, criticises the coquetry of women when they attended public worship in wearing these head veils, "perfectly transparent and slightly ornamented with embroidery." These veils were the prototypes of the mantillas at present worn by women in southern countries of Europe.

Fig. 24.—Figure from an Etruscan tomb at Vulci.

Phrygia.—From the shores of Phrygia, Asiatic and Babylonian embroideries were shipped for Greece and Italy. The Romans denominated such embroideries *phrygionæ*, and the embroiderer *phrygio.* Stuffs woven with gold were called *chrysoclavum,* * or *auro-clavum,*† but golden embroideries were specified as *auriphrygium.* This word is the root of the French word *orfroi,* a title commonly applied to the golden bands which adorn copes, chasubles, and other ecclesiastical vestments.

The greater number of the early embroideries used in Greece and at Rome came, as a rule, from Asia; the patterns on them were Oriental in character. When a conqueror

* From the Greek χρυσός, gold.

† The *clavus* was, according to the majority of authorities who have written about it, a band of ornamental weaving or embroidery to embellish the tunic. There was a broad band, the *latus clavus,* and a narrow one, the *angustus clavus.* The term *chrysoclavus* might apply to either, and would merely imply a golden band. It is not therefore a term peculiarly descriptive of woven stuffs.

returned with the honours of his victories thick upon him, he was invested with a *toga palmata*, or robe embroidered by Phrygians with palm devices, probably similar in form to those frequently used on Cashmere shawls, and not to be mistaken for an ornament of classic style peculiar to Rome or Athens. The Oriental origin of such embroidered robes appears to be undisputed. Whenever some distinguishing mark was required for a vestment, embroidery was called upon to supply it.

The mother of the Maccabees wishing to arouse her sons' courage upon their departure for battle, gave them white linen robes, and on taking leave of them said, " These maternal fingers spun this thread, with which they likewise wove and embroidered these garments ; may they become either your standards should you vanquish the foes of your God and country, or your shrouds should you fall victims to the steel of the faithless ! "

Like other arts, that of the needle has often given form to the sentiments of the human heart, and its progress has kept pace with that of architecture, painting, and sculpture. Its expressions, like theirs, occur throughout all phases in the history of civilization.

Summary.—Thus we have found that embroidery has held sway during ancient times. Egyptians and Asiatic nations, from Babylonians, Hebrews, Phrygians, to Indians and Chinese, have displayed high skill in its practice. Greeks and Romans who rank foremost in the ancient history of Europe adopted various processes for embroidery from Orientals, remaining nevertheless their inferiors in skill, as is more or less shown by the importations from Asia of the more sumptuous and

golden embroideries which alone were deemed worthy
for occasions of stately triumphs.

As regards the kinds of threads successively employed for embroidery, it will be remembered that silk
was the latest to become known in Europe. At the
period of Christ's dispensation, with which this chapter
closes, embroideries had been made chiefly with woollen,
cotton, and flaxen threads, though often intermixed with
strands of gold and silver, China at this period being
almost the only country enjoying free use of silk.

The patterns rendered in ancient embroideries were
based upon flowers, trees, and animals, the latter sometimes in processional series. In more important embroideries hunting scenes and combats were displayed,
whilst others were depicted, with forms of divinities,
typical of stars, natural forces, and elements. To the
Greeks the gods were omnipresent ; but to the Hebrews
such familiar emblems of the divinity were unknown,
and they used nought but cherubim. Ornamental
devices were simple in character, and derived largely
from architectural enrichments. From the point of
view of ordinary usage, it would seem that at the
periods we cursorily allude to, embroideries were
rarities, highly esteemed, and employed exclusively in
the adornment of the temple or the palace, of priests or
persons of high degree.

Unfortunately at the present day we possess no
specimens with which we might verify the descriptions
of them put forward in the works of noted Greek and
Roman writers. Nothing exists of the peplos of
Minerva of Athens, of a Phrygian chlamys worn by
some Roman noble, of those famous embroideries tell-

ing of the exploits of Greeks and Trojans, or of the celebrated veils and hangings of the Temple.

In fact, beyond fragments of mummy cloths from Egyptian tombs, we scarcely possess any relics of textile fabrics produced prior to the Christian era.*

* The excavations of burial grounds at Akhmîm in Upper Egypt have brought to light various pieces of embroidery of the Roman period, from the first to fourth centuries A.D. M. Maspero considers that the textiles discovered at Akhmîm are nearly all of the Coptic period. Some, however, are earlier. Among such may be instanced an extremely fine specimen of flax cloth embroidered with brilliant coloured worsteds in a sort of darning stitch so as to make the embroidery on the front of the flax consist of large loops. This piece has been presented by the Rev. Greville Chester to the British Museum. The design is Roman, and represents a boat in which are a Cupid and Venus (?). The border is of rich flower and leafy garlands. Other pieces of Roman embroidery of the same date, but done in crewel and chain stitch, are in the South Kensington Museum.

CHAPTER III.

FROM THE CHRISTIAN ERA TO THE CRUSADES.

At the commencement of our era the boundaries of the Roman empire extended over all then known countries; and civilisation, commerce, and knowledge of industrial processes with which the barbarians had hitherto been unacquainted, gradually developed in them.

So far as embroidery is concerned we have to bear in mind two distinct movements. On the one hand, wealth and luxury centred themselves first in Rome under the Cæsars and Antonines, and later in Byzantium, when Constantine made it his metropolis in the fourth century. On the other hand, an active commerce was established by the East with those Western nations which were governed originally by Roman proconsuls, and subsequently by their first kings, who gradually freed their kingdoms from Roman domination.

Once instructed by Oriental importations, handicraftsmen of France, Spain, England, and Germany, set themselves to produce embroidery, which for a considerable period, however, bore strong traces of Oriental influence. At length native artificers ventured to draw inspiration for their ornaments from things amongst which they dwelt, and thus, in the art of embroidery, as with their architecture, they created locally distinctive styles.

And now, recurring to the history of embroidery as it opens with the Christian era, we may briefly mention the tradition that the Virgin Mary, when told by the angel Gabriel of her Divine conception, embroidered a veil, such probably as she herself might wear on going to the Temple.

But the early Christians, almost always subject to persecution, were little addicted to the vanities of embroidery. Perret, in his work on the *Catacombs of Rome*, calls attention to several paintings of costume ornamented with *callicules*, or bits of brightly coloured stuffs cut into circles or squares which were sewn (*appliqués*) on to the breast or skirt of the tunic (fig. 25). Such pieces of *appliqué* work were used for a long time as the only ornaments of priests' albs. Comparatively insignificant as they

Fig. 25.—Engraving taken from the *Catacombes de Rome*.

appear from the catacomb paintings to have been, it is important to refer to them, since from them indirectly were developed the gorgeous orphreys with panels of broidery which we shall often be called upon to consider in our investigations of embroidered ecclesiastical vestments.

The court of Roman emperors must have constantly furnished costly commissions to be executed by those who devoted themselves to the art of the needle. It was often a season of pompous and unstinted extravagance one indeed when representations of all sorts and public games were leading factors in the government of a people: *Panem et circenses.*

The Emperor Augustus, rivalling the splendours of Antony and Cleopatra in Egypt, imported, for his festivals and triumphs in Rome, enormous quantities of embroidered stuffs from Persia, and probably too from China.

Metellus Scipio purchased during his consulate (B.C. 52—46), at the price of eight hundred thousand sesterces (about £6,700), marvellous covers for couches of Babylonian embroidery, *triclinaria Babylonica*, which, a hundred years later, the Emperor Nero acquired at the enormous price of four millions of sesterces (£160,000).

Was the immense velarium stretched by Nero across the Colosseum at Rome worked in embroidery, or was it of tapestry-weaving as Mr. Eugène Müntz suggests? Upon it were represented the starry firmament and Apollo driving a chariot drawn by steeds. All seems to point to the conclusion that, in view of the considerable time which the tapestry-weaving of such an enormous hanging would have required, it is more likely that embroidery, as a far readier and speedier process, was called into operation.

Lampridius describes the exquisite table napkins embroidered for the Emperor Heliogabalus, successor to Caligula in A.D. 217; upon them were displayed all the dainties and viands that could be wanted for a feast. However easily embroidered, the effect of such things can scarcely have been artistic. It responded, however, to Roman taste, for, as M. Müntz says, the tendency of Roman art was more towards rich and gaudy display than elegance and beauty. Such an influence also discernible in costumes is an evidence of that degenerate taste which potently manifested itself after the reign of the Antonines.

For many centuries senators had worn a white toga bordered with two purple bands (*clavi*); but under the empire as many as seven bands would be worked on the toga, and in time came to be made of gold thread only, consequently they were termed *auri clavi*.

Until the middle of the third century the emperors disdained effeminate ornaments, and were content with a simple purple toga. But Aurelian (270—275) adopted for his toga a style of splendour worthy of an Oriental monarch; rich stuffs, with gold and pearls, were used by this fierce warrior.

Diocletian (284—305) even surpassed such pomp of display which thenceforth became a leading attribute of the imperial dignity. The term of each emperor's reign became shortened; the enjoyments accompanying it were of brief duration; and rapidly executed processes such as embroidery were necessary to meet the pressing and changeful demands of the times, which under calmer circumstances might have been met by weaving. Under such pressure embroidery is more readily produced than weavings, and so the shuttle was, in these circumstances, completely superseded by the needle. Embroidery could be used not only for ornamenting costumes to which it is so appropriate, but it would also supplant monumental tapestry-weaving.

The great wealth of embroidery used at Rome

during imperial times was outshone by that in Byzantium, when Constantine settled his seat of government there. Contiguous, so to speak, with Asiatic opulence, the courts of Byzantine emperors knew no limits for their extravagances. In Charles Bayet's *Byzantine Art*, says Francisque Michel,[*] one may read descriptions of stuffs produced in imitation of those imported from Asia. Amongst them would be seen "griffins, basilisks, unicorns, lions, tigers, elephants, eagles, peacocks, and other birds, intermingled with large and small circular bands or medallion shapes, golden apples, palms, shrubs, and flowers." Byzantine records, constantly, give such titles as the following, which recur again and again during the Middle Ages : *Pallia cum rotæ*, stuffs decorated with wheels or circular bands; *stuculata*, with lozengy diapering ; *quadrapula, exapula, octapula*, with panels four-sided, hexagonal, octagonal, etc. ; *virgata*, with stripes ; *cum bestiis et avibus*, with beasts and birds ; as well as *cum historia*, representations of Biblical and mythological subjects.

Embroidery used in working the fabrics storied with incidents from the New Testament, presented all that the ingenious imagination of Byzantine artists pictured, in order to pictorially elucidate the Gospels which at that time were fascinating and influencing human thought. Subjects such as these were worked into the great draperies then in common use, for hanging between colonnades and porches of palaces and churches. The heavy stuffs of which these were made were more suited to the weight

* Francisque Michel, *Recherches sur les Étoffes de Soie*.

of Byzantine embroidery than were articles of clothing.

Nothing, however, if we may rely upon contemporary accounts, contributed as much to most artfully wrought embroidery as the devotion in making altar and liturgical cloths; Paul the Silentiary * describes one which was used on the altar in the church of St. Sophia; it was "embroidered in the centre with the figure of Christ robed in a purple tunic and golden mantle of dazzling effulgence; in His left hand He held the book of the Gospels, His right hand being stretched forth. On either side, clad in white, were St. Peter, with the Book of Holy Writ, and St. Paul, with a gold staff surmounted by a cross. Along the borders were representations of miracles and diverse incidents of sacred history, amongst which the flattering artist had depicted the Emperor Justinian and his wife distributing alms to the churches."

Such subjects admirably beseemed their sacred service. But this was no longer the case when scenes from the New Testament were used in the decoration of secular costume. A mosaic in the church of St. Vitale, at Ravenna, displays the Empress Theodora † wearing a cloak embroidered with the adoration of the Magi. Following the fashion of the court, rich persons adopted sacred subjects for the embroidery on their costumes; one senator boasts six hundred figures upon his robes of state! Abuses of this class lead us to a just sense of that righteous indignation fulminated

---

* Paul the Silentiary, *Description of St. Sophia*, verse 755 *et seq.*

† See Reproductions of Mosaics in South Kensington Museum; also in M. Gerspach's work on *Mosaics*, p. 63.

by Asterius, Bishop of Amasus, in Pontus, against the vainglorious "who wore the Gospels upon their backs instead of in their hearts. Every one," he says, "is eager to clothe himself, his wife, and his children with stuffs ornamented with flowers and numberless figures, and to such an extent is this done, that when the wealthy classes show themselves in public, little children gather round in crowds and point their fingers at them, making merry at their expense. On such raiments are to be seen lions, panthers, bears, bulls, dogs, forests, rocks, hunters, all, in fact, that painters can copy from nature. It is not sufficient to adorn walls in this manner, for tunics and mantles are also covered with similar decorations. The more religious of the wealthy classes require artists to supply them with subjects taken at their suggestion from the New Testament, Jesus Christ and His disciples, or else His many miracles," etc.

This language marks the important, though often undoubtedly exaggerated, consideration bestowed upon embroidery during the Byzantine empire. A favourite scheme of arrangement in Byzantine patterns was that in which occurred pairs of animals or birds, confronted and separated by the *hom*, the sacred tree of the Persians, a sort of palm adopted as a symbol in the religion of Zoroaster, who called it the tree of life. Constantly recurrent in the Middle Ages this *motif* is to be found in woven textiles and designs for embroidery which will be hereafter described.

Silk now became an article of regular trade in the Western markets. The Chinese were always ready to deliver any quantities of woven silks, but they jealously protected any western importation of silkworms, in the rearing of which they virtually enjoyed a monopoly. The Emperor Justinian accordingly devised a stratagem to counteract this, by securing the services of two Persian monks, long resident in the far East, who visited Byzantium and undertook to bring thither silkworms from China. One of the grounds which recommended their scheme to the emperor was that by it "the Romans would no longer be under the necessity of importing silk from their enemies the Persians, or from any other nation." These itinerant monks forthwith returned to "Serinda" (possibly China), and having procured a store of silkworm eggs, they concealed them in the hollow of their bamboo staves, to evade the jealous vigilance of the Chinese, and so returned with them to Byzantium.* The rearing of the worms was undertaken forthwith in Asia Minor and Greece, and later in Central Europe.

The costliness of the materials, the complication of the designs, and the strivings after effects of solid reliefs, frequently led Byzantine embroiderers far away from canons of good taste. Costumes loaded with embroideries of this nature lost suppleness, and hung in rigid, straight folds, surrounding the wearers of them with sumptuous encumbrances.† At the same time it must not be overlooked that the Byzantines embroidered

* See Yates' *Textrinum Antiquorum*, p. 231, where a quotation from Procopius' *De Bello Gothico*, iv., 17, is given. Lady Marian Alford, in her valuable book *Needlework as Art*, names Cosmas Indicopleutes, the Indian navigator and monk, who wrote an account of his journeys as one of the two Persian monks. But neither Gibbon, vol. vii., p. 97, *et seq.*, nor Yates so speak of him.

† Eug. Müntz, *History of Tapestry*.

figure subjects in a most remarkable manner; and these very properly received the highest admiration when they passed into the hands of other peoples.

Apparently there are no remains extant of Byzantine embroideries produced before the seventh century. We must, nevertheless, not omit to mention certain textile specimens preserved in the Hermitage at St. Petersburg, one of which is described as a purple worsted stuff embroidered with green and yellow palmates, and exhumed from a tomb of the third century A.D.[*]

Amongst other articles made at Byzantium were state trappings and gala harness for horses, to which the heavy relief embroideries were well adapted. St. Chrysostom speaks of wealthy persons who provided their horses " with trimmings of sparkling gold work suited for women's wear ;" and Oriental courts of the present day have scarcely modified such splendour in the paraphernalia of their horses and elephants. Gold is used for them, not only in threads and fringes, but also as plates or plaques, fitted into the leather or other material ; intermixed are spangles, jewels, glass trinkets, of all colours and sizes. The fringes are similarly treated, and glitter and sparkle to the pawing of the bedizened steeds. All this clinquant finery glistens in the public places beneath the rays of the Oriental sun, producing the effect of boundless affluence so consonant with the majesty of a sovereign.

[*] In the *Compte Rendu de la Commission Imperiale Archéologique* (1878-9), facsimile illustrations of these precious examples are given ; and full descriptions of them by Stephani are contained in the accompanying text. They were taken in the course of excavations in 1875-6 from the tomb of the "Seven Brothers" near Temriouk in the Province of Koudan, which includes the south-east corner of the Sea of

In the seventh century the rise of Mohammedan power began to impair the mightiness of the Byzantine court. But the triumph of the Mussulman, far from

Azof. From various data Stephani convincingly fixes their date at the fourth and third centuries B.C., not A.D. as Mons. Lefebure appears

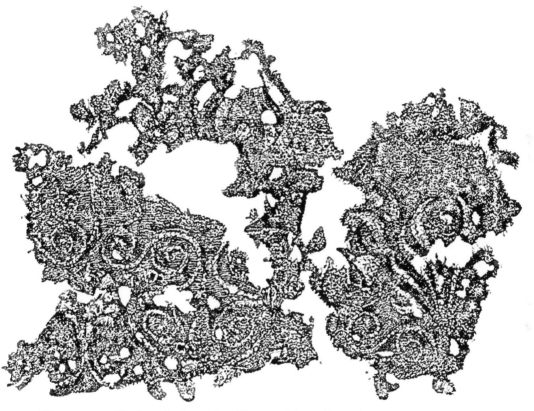

Fig. 25A.—Chain stitch embroidery with yellow flax upon mulberry-coloured worsted material. Greek. Fourth century B.C. From tomb of the Seven Brothers, near Temriouk, in the province of Kouban.

to think. The specimen here engraved is worked apparently with a silky-looking flax thread, yellow in colour, in chain stitch on a blue-red worsted material. In other relics of this important find we have thin golden plates shaped like leaves stitched to worsted stuff; and the patterns of others are worked in short stitches. The embroidery displays clear evidence of a complete knowledge, in the fourth century B.C., on the part of the Greeks, of these stitches, which, as might be expected, were evidently wrought with a comparatively cumbrous needle.

injuring textile arts, so intimately wedded with Oriental
fashions, infused into them the spirit of a new departure.

The costumes of the Caliphs become dreamlike wonders to all who attempt to describe them. All sorts of
leather articles were embroidered, not only saddles and
harness, but also red morocco leather boots, scabbards
of swords and daggers, are often exquisite works of the
embroiderer's art.

But what shall be said of the carpets and hangings?
Whether they were woven or embroidered, our admiring astonishment has been won for centuries by
their colouring, which has never been excelled.

Leading a nomad life, the Arab frequently embroidered the tent of his chieftain. When the Caliph
Haroun-al-Raschid sent presents to Charlemagne in 802,
amongst them were magnificent and precious textiles,
and a chief's tent superbly embroidered.

As in previous times, the Kaaba at Mecca was always
hung with the richest of tissues; and whosoever of
the faithful could offer the finer and rarer pieces was
accorded the privilege of decorating the tomb of the
Prophet Mahomet. In 776 the mere weight of these
offerings hanging upon the supports of the temple
threatened its stability. The columns were hidden
beneath the masses of them. The greater number of
these hangings had wide borderings of flowers and
sprays interlacing themselves with the noble and picturesque lettering of the prayers of Islam, embroidered
upon the green ground sacred to the prophet.

Such customs survive to the present day, and the
sanctuary is always covered with a huge scroll on

which are embroidered verses from the Koran. Each year, on the occasion of the pilgrimage to Mecca, the curtain in use is replaced by a new one brought from Egypt upon the back of a camel dedicated to the service. The pilgrims rend the old curtain into pieces and preserve them as holy relics.

It must not be supposed that embroidery became extinct with the decay of the Byzantine empire; the Greeks maintained the best traditions of the art.

The difficulty of determining whether the different specimens described by Byzantine authors were of tapestry weaving or of needlework, is freely acknowledged in his *History of Tapestry Making*, by M. Müntz. He adds, however, with good reason, that "amongst the different textile processes in use, one only was universally known and employed from one end to the other of Europe, and that was embroidery. And Byzantium held for many centuries the foremost place as the producer of the richest and most perfected examples of the art."

The contentions of the Iconoclasts drove many Byzantine artists into Italy. The *Liber Pontificalis*, or Chronicle of the Popes, written in 687 by Athanasius the librarian, contains mention of an influx into Rome of gorgeous embroideries, the work of men who had arrived from Greece and Constantinople.

The Treasury at Ratisbon in Bavaria includes a Byzantine embroidery, which probably is a work of this period, and is certainly very remarkable. It was found in the tomb of Gunther, who died, Bishop of Bamberg, in 1062 (fig. 26). Upon it is depicted the Emperor Constantine as master of the world, riding on a white

4

palfrey and receiving homage from the East and West,
personified as the two Romes under the guise of two
queens, wearing mural crowns, and humbly offering to
the monarch a warrior's helmet on the one hand and a

Fig. 26.--Byzantine embroidery from the tomb of Gunther, Bishop of
Bamberg, preserved at Ratisbon.

crown of peace on the other.   In all respects this specimen is noteworthy for the dignified pose of the figures
and the distinctness of definition imparted to them by
careful and precise execution.   It possesses as much

style in the higher sense of the word as the finest of Byzantine mosaics.

Leaving Byzantium and her magnificence we now turn our attention to examples of simpler and more artless work, notable for a certain purity of sentiment, and made by Western countries.

With our Gallic forefathers embroidery was an old established art. Pliny affirms that they were skilful " in embroidering carpets, in making felt with wool, and in using the waste to make mattresses, the invention of which is due to them."

Under Roman government the Gauls may be said to have first enjoyed the advantages of civilization and the pleasures of its attendant arts, which were developed under the Merovingian and Carlovingian kings, by the latter of whom abbeys were built all over the country. These establishments infused new life into a practice of the arts generally, including, of course, embroidery.

The Romans were conquerors ; fortifying towns, and carrying on great public works, but paying scant heed to commerce. The later Greeks, on the contrary, were merchants and navigators, closely following the heels of their soldiery, and making use of the resources opened to them ; they monopolized trade between the East and those countries through which the conquering Romans had constructed great highways, as through the forests of Gaul and Germany. Lading their vessels at Phrygian ports, notably at Gaza, with merchandize brought by caravans from Southern Palestine, the land of Media, and the kingdom of the Sabæans of Yemen, they transported it to the Island of Delos, where, according to Festus and Strabo, they founded the most flourishing market in the world. On the backs of men or mules the goods were further distributed to populous centres.

Pilgrimages to the tombs of saints gave rise to the periodical holding of large fairs; under the reign of Dagobert, Greek merchants came to France to dispose of their goods at the fairs established at the instance of his minister, St. Eloi, in the plain du Landit; close to the abbey in course of erection over the shrine of St. Denis.

Not only commerce, but industry as well, focussed itself about the monasteries. As Mignet cogently remarks in his *Historical Studies* :—" Monasteries were the workshops in which the traditions of ancient arts were maintained and perpetuated."

The art of writing manuscripts, and of sumptuously illuminating them, was specially nurtured in the cloisters; and the drawing, colouring, and gilding of these splendid productions provided embroiderers with seductive patterns for their needles. The famous monastery of St. Gall in Switzerland contained important workrooms for weavers and embroiderers. Bishops and abbots stimulated the fabrication of ornamental tissues to enhance the resplendency of ecclesiastical ritual. Gregory of Tours, in his *History of the Franks,* which covers a period from 417 to 591, frequently mentions kindred fabrics, used as hangings for the church walls. St. Yriex in his will speaks of them as *Velola per ipsius oratorii parietes,* curtains for the walls of the chapel.

Funerals also were occasions for great displays : richly embroidered coverings, or palls, were placed over the dead when exposed for the veneration of crowds. The mortuary cloth of King Childeric was embroidered with three hundred golden bees.

The religious episodes of the Old Testament more frequently reproduced were Samson slaying the lion, and Daniel in the lions' den; these having been adopted by the primitive Church to symbolize the fights and persecutions of which the martyrs had been forced to pay the penalty; * whilst the Trinity, the Annunciation and the Adoration of the Shepherds and the Magi were selected from the New Testament for similar purposes.

These embroideries were usually worked on linen ground, with either worsteds or silks; for superior qualities, gold threads were sparingly used. The stitches employed were satin stitch, the simplest of all; feather stitch (long and short stitch); and couching : † the ground upon which these were worked showed itself between the various forms of the pattern.

Authors often write of cloths "*acu pictæ*," painted with the needle, a capital expression to define the characteristic *rôle* which embroidery played in those times.

Patterns of crosses surrounded by circles were often embroidered on stuffs, and were termed "*stauracis*" from the Greek σταυρός, a cross; mention of these devices occurs in the *Liber Pontificalis*, and in a letter

* These broideries were called *leonata*, ornamental lion-subjects.

† Couching is laying threads upon a material, and then stitching them down to it by small stitches. There are varieties of couching, but the more elaborate of them are those in which gold threads are stitched down in such a way as to produce an effect like delicate golden wicker plaiting, or one of diaper patterns upon a golden ground.

from Pope Paul I. to Pepin the Short A.D. 757 (fig. 32).

The wealth of sacerdotal ornaments, made in monasteries, throws a light upon the power and authority enjoyed by the bishops. As popular protectors of all subject to despotic acts of lords and kings, as mitigators of harsh justice meted out by princes, the bishops wielded the highest moral power. Richer and richer as ornament was bestowed upon their vestments, so was respect increased for the solemn and important rites of which they were the ministrants. Embroidery was the fostering auxiliary of outward impressiveness in the ceremonials of the Church, and was lavished upon copes, chasubles, and dalmatics.

The peculiar use of these ornate accessories was determined by councils. The cope was the vestment worn in public processions, and to it was attached a hood, known originally as the *pluvial*, because it protected its wearer from the rain.

At the office of the Mass the officiating priest wore a chasuble, "*casula*," and the deacon a dalmatic.

A mitre is worn by a bishop; the band along its lower edge was termed the "*circulus*," and encircled the head. Another band placed vertically in the centre of the front of the mitre was called the "*titulus*," both would be of rich embroidery, studded with precious stones.

At his consecration, a bishop is invested with a pair of gloves on which religious emblems are worked in colours or gold.

The episcopal shoes of the prelate are always embroidered, and early specimens of these are preserved amongst the relics of clerical apparel in many sacristies of old cathedrals.

From this period onwards we have a much more exact knowledge of the embroideries then made, and we are not, as in respect of those of very ancient times, thrown back upon the writings only of authors. Museums, church treasuries, and private collections supply us with authentic objects, from the study of which we can trace the various stages in the artistic development of embroidery.

The museum of tapestries at Florence claims to own " *Vela di pieta* " which belonged to Dagobert in the seventh century, as well as embroidered Auxerre cloths of the year 840.

Excavations of tombs of saints and bishops of this period have brought to light fragments of embroidery, and amongst them that very precious piece of work now deposited in the treasury at Tongres. Another found at Troyes is figured with serpents and birds enriched with little plaques of gold.

A cope of red silk presented by Charlemagne is to be seen in the cathedral of Metz. Upon it, wrought in yellow, blue, and green threads, are great eagles with outstretched wings and claws being gnawed by monsters, depicted in a fine style.

A thorough study of costume at the time of Charlemagne (767—814) may be made from the life of this great emperor written by a contemporary monk of St. Gall, Eginhard,* of which Guizot has given us a new edition. The following extract tells us " that on solemn occasions of pomp Charlemagne wore a close-fitting

* Eginhard, *Vita Karolis imperatoris.*

vest or jacket of gold embroidery, sandals, or, more properly speaking, slippers set with precious stones, a cloak or mantle fastened by a golden brooch or *fibula*, and a diadem of gold glistening with gems ; on other occasions his costume differed little from that of ordinary mortals."*

This great monarch gave all encouragement to the

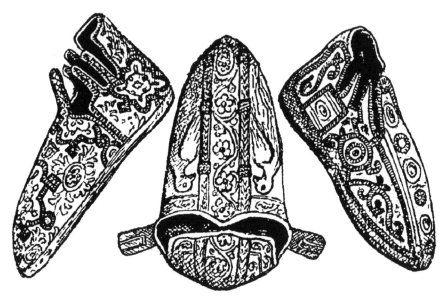

Fig. 27.- -Embroidered Slippers that belonged to Charlemagne ; in the Treasury at St. Denis, Paris.

arts ; and the princesses of his court, from his mother Bertha of the large feet to his daughters, were sedulous in becoming proficients in the art of embroidery. A chronicler writes,—

> *Ses filles fist bien doctriner*
> *Et apprendre keudre et filer.*†

St. Giselle, Bertha's sister, founded many convents

---

* At Aix-la-Chapelle and Nuremberg there are vestments said to have been worn by Charlemagne.

† *Chronique Rimée* by Philippe Mouskés.

in Aquitaine and Provence, and taught their inmates all sorts of needlework.

Eagles were the most frequently used ornamental motives in the embroideries of Charlemagne's reign, which were hence called " *aquilata.*" Eagles thus became the insignia of the Western empire. From the royal capital of Aix-la-Chapelle they disseminated themselves throughout Germany, and were adopted as heraldic bearings by the various royal houses.

Several princesses subsequently to the Carlovingian period distinguished themselves as adepts in the art of embroidery. Judith, mother of Charles the Bald, and godmother to Harold, King of Denmark, who, with his family came to Ingelheim in 826 to be there baptised, embroidered and bejewelled a mantle for His Majesty's use on this occasion.

Adélaïs, consort of Hugh Capet (987—996), presented the church of St. Martin at Tours with a cope, on the back of which she had embroidered the Deity, surrounded by seraphim and cherubim, the front being adorned with an Adoration of the Lamb of God.

But the name which dominates above all others is that of Queen Mathilda. Of her many embroideries it is true that one only, a cloth of the class " *acu pictæ,*" survives to the present day, its importance having arrested the attention of all historians.

This famous needlework is now preserved in the Bayeux (Calvados) Museum. Tradition, apparently well supported, attributes its production to Queen Mathilda, wife of William the Conqueror, who died in 1087. Certain critics have held that this work was done by his grand-daughter, the Empress Mathilda, widow in

1125 of Henry V., Emperor of Germany, and wife, by her second marriage, of Geoffroy, Count of Anjou. In any case, the embroidery clearly manifests the influence of those who were fully cognisant with, if they did not actually take part in, the incidents displayed throughout a narrow linen band over two hundred feet long. The work must have been in hand some years before it was completed.

It is, according to the old chroniclers, " *Une tente très longue et estroite de telle à broderies de ymages et escriptaux faisant représentation du Conquest de l'Angleterre.*" Its exact dimensions are 70·34 metres long by 0·50 metre wide.

The material is of stout linen, upon which appear persons, horses, ships, etc., in all one thousand two hundred and fifty-five figures, worked in worsted threads, laid upon the surface of the linen, and held to it by means of cross stitches taken over them into the ground. The colours of the worsteds, although fantastically matched, sufficiently express the desired effects. The interpolated inscriptions explain different episodes connected with the Conquest of England by the Normans. They commence with Harold leaving the Court of Edward the Confessor, and finish with the Battle of Hastings. The whole work, in fact, is a sort of needle-wrought epic. The drawing of the figures is perhaps infantile, but the work has the charm of frankness and irrefragable authenticity.*

It has been misnamed a tapestry, since it is entirely

---

* See *The Bayeux Tapestry*, by Frank Rede Fowke, published 1875. (Arundel Society.)

an embroidery done with the needle by means of couched worsteds on linen (fig. 28).

After the Battle of Hastings William the Conqueror is said to have held a meeting with the nobles of his new kingdom, presenting himself before them in a mantle covered with Anglo-Saxon embroideries. Is it probable that this robe is the same as that mentioned in the inventory of the Bayeux Cathedral, A.D. 1476, after the entry relating to the *broderie à telle* repre-

Fig. 28.—Piece of the Bayeux embroidery.

senting the Conquest of England? Two mantles are there described, one of King William, "all of gold, powdered with crosses and blossoms of gold, and edged along the lower border with an orphrey of figures; and a mantle said to have been worn by the duchess, all powdered with little figures, and trimmed in front with orphreys."

These robes have usually been thought to be of English work, and it is certain that, at the time, England was noted for her embroideries.

In the seventh century St. Etheldreda, first Abbess

of the Monastery at Ely, made an offering to St. Cuthbert of a sacred ornament she had worked with gold thread and precious stones.*   At Durham are preserved the cope and maniple belonging to St. Cuthbert and found in his tomb; they are considered to be specimens of *opus Anglicum*.

Mrs. Bury Palliser writes, that in the year 800 Denbart, Bishop of Durham, allotted the income from a farm of two hundred acres, for life, to an embroideress named Eanswitha, in consideration of her looking after, mending, and, when necessary, renewing the vestments of the clergy in his diocese.

The battle-standard of King Alfred (871—900) is reputed to have been embroidered with the figure of a splendid crow by Danish princesses. Edgitha, wife of Edward the Confessor (1041—1066), was noted for her skilful needlework : whilst the Anglo-Saxon Gudric, sometime Sheriff of Buckingham, gave Alcuid a piece of land on condition that she instructed his daughter in embroidery.

Facts like these explain the reason for such punctilious records of old embroideries as that of a tunic embroidered at Winchester by the wife of one Alderet, which Queen Mathilda bequeathed to the abbey of the Holy Trinity at Caen. This queen also gave to the abbey a golden cloak to be made up into a cope, as well as her waistband of gold, ornamented with emblems, which should be used for suspending the lantern before the high altar.

Harold's gift to the monastery of Croyland, of a

---

* *St. Cuthbert : An Account of the State in which his Remains were Found*, by Rev. J. Raine (Durham : 1828).

parchment worked in gold, with a representation of the siege of Troy, possibly indicates the king's literary and artistic taste. M. de Ronchaud remarks how closely the tradition of Helen's embroideries during the siege of Troy find an analogy with that of the great epic embroidered by Mathilda in respect of the Conquest of England.*

But it may be asked, What is the *opus Anglicum* above mentioned? Mrs. Bury Palliser furnishes an answer.† "Happily," she writes, "we possess in the cope of the monastery of Syon, now pre-

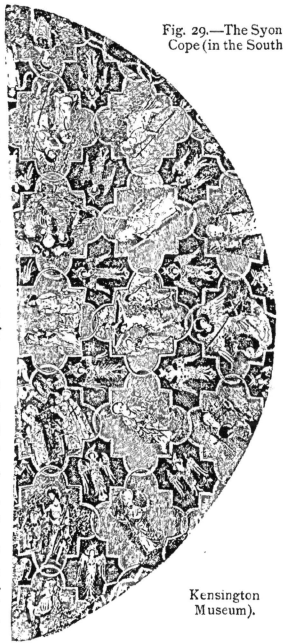

Fig. 29.—The Syon Cope (in the South Kensington Museum).

---

* *La Tapisserie dans l'Antiquite*, by Ronchaud.

† *Encyclopædia Britannica* (Edinburgh: 1878), vol. viii., p. 162. See also *Textile Fabrics*, by Canon Rock (1870), Introduction, p. 98; *Cantor Lectures*, by Alan S. Cole (1886), p. 31.

served in the South Kensington Museum, an invaluable
specimen of this *opus Anglicum*, or English embroidery
of the thirteenth century. The greater portion of its
design is worked in a chain stitch (tambour or crochet),
especially in the faces of the figures where the stitch
begins in the centre say of a cheek, and is then worked
in a spiral, thus forming a series of circular lines. The
texture so obtained is then, by means of a hot, small,
and round-knobbed iron, pressed into indentations at
the centre of each spiral, and an effect of relief imparted
to it."* Following Canon Rock, she concludes that
this is the distinctive feature of *opus Anglicum*. But
the conclusion is arrived at apparently without sufficient data; chain stitch may perhaps have been invented by some ingenious Anglo-Saxon embroideress
who used a hooked instead of the ordinary needle. It
is more probable, however, that English needlewomen
did not restrict their embroidery to chain-stitch work
only : they were likely to have been acquainted with all
the stitches commonly in use at the time, and they
certainly produced many embroideries with pearls and
with beads such as were then made in Scotland.
Indeed, Mrs. Palliser hardly seems quite assured that
opus Anglicum meant chain-stitch work only, for she
terminates her remarks by saying that *opus Plumarium*,
or feather (long and short) stitch, was also frequently
used.

However this may be, the Syon Cope is a specimen

* It may be here noted that work done in chain stitch in spirals
(and this arrangement of stitches is frequent in certain Persian embroideries from Resht, etc,) assumes an undulating surface without the application of any such tooling as that imagined by Canon
Rock and Mrs. Palliser.

of the very highest interest. The illustration we give shows the Crucifixion with the Virgin and St. John at the foot of the Cross in the centre. Above is the Redeemer uprisen, crowned as a king, and seated on a cushioned throne with the Virgin Mary. Below we find the Archangel Michael slaying the dragon, whilst on the right and left of these are incidents from the history

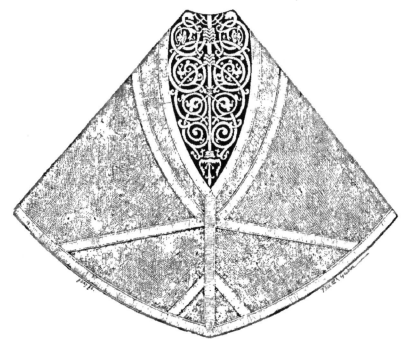

Fig. 30.—Chasuble of St. Thomas of Canterbury at Sens.

of the death and burial of the Virgin, the Resurrection, and various Apostles. Each subject is set in quatrefoils, between which are cherubim or angels standing on wheels.

It is evident that the cope has been cut from a large embroidery. The outer borders to it (which we have omitted) are of slightly later date, and are wrought with armorial bearings, with coloured silks, and gold and silver threads in small cross stitches.* The whole, however, is undoubtedly the finest specimen extant of *opus Anglicum* in its wider sense.

St. Dunstan, the artistic English monk of the twelfth century, has been cited as a designer for embroideries. Anglo-Saxon calligraphists are usually considered to be the originators of those sumptuously illuminated letters, in which a profusion of dragon-headed scrolls and interlacing twists is seen. There was therefore no lack in the eighth to twelfth centuries of clever designers and skilful workwomen, who might well found the reputation of an *opus Anglicum*.

Fig. 31.—Details from the stole of St. Thomas of Canterbury.

In M. de Caumont's and M. Gaussen's books illustrations are given of a fine chasuble (fig. 30) and stole (fig. 31), and a mitre worn by St. Thomas à Becket, who was martyred at Canterbury on the 29th December, 1170. The originals are preserved in the cathedral of Sens. The pattern about the neck and shoulders is to some extent based upon the interlaced scroll forms used by Anglo-Saxon MS. illuminators.

In the treasury of the cathedral at Namur is the mitre worn by Bishop Jacques de Vitry, who died in

* This description of the Syon Cope is adapted from that given in the *Descriptive Catalogue of the Collections of Tapestry and Embroidery in the South Kensington Museum*, 1887.

1244.* It is a mass of embroideries in gold and silver threads, with a figure of St. Lawrence on the front, and one of St. Thomas of Canterbury on the back. A very similar mitre is in the museum at Munich.

According to the Rev. J. Raine, chasubles of red silk (taffetas), thickly embroidered and enriched with gold leaves, bezants, and pearls, were found at the death of Hugh Pudsey, Bishop of Durham, in 1194.

The splendid vestments and ornaments worn by the English clergy who visited Rome in 1246 were so highly admired by Pope Innocent IV. that he ordered similar articles from Cistercian monasteries in England. Amongst them, perhaps, were two copes now in the Vatican, which bear a close resemblance to the Syon Cope.

St. Henry (Emperor of Germany from 973 to 1024) presented an embroidery to the cathedral at Ratisbon, which the learned archæologists, Cahier and Martin, have classed as *opus Anglicum*. His Imperial Majesty's taste for fine embroideries led him to give a magnificent piece of work to St. Peter's at Rome.

St. Etienne, King of Hungary, also admired embroidery. His wife, Gisela, organized weaving and embroidery workrooms near the palace, whence originated the celebrated *point de Hongrie* (Hungary stitch), a name which to this day is applied to embroideries with a ground of zigzag lines. This queen is held to have made the ecclesiastical vestment which was preserved in the abbey of St. Arnold near Metz. It was given by Pope Leo IX. when he officiated at the consecration (5th October, 1049) of the church, newly

* Didron, *Annales archéologiques.*

erected by the monks of St. Arnold. It is described as a chasuble of crimson satin, shot with blue like the breast of a wood-pigeon. On its lower portion was embroidered a shrub, with branches evenly displayed, and surmounted by two birds confronted ; this group shaped itself into a lozenge or diamond, and similar groups were worked about it. The chasuble was circular, with an opening for the head in the centre. From this opening a purple band, ·80 metre wide, descended down the front and back ; on the front was wrought in gold a figure of Christ, blessing with His right hand and holding the Gospels in His left, with St. Peter above Him and St. Paul below, a design which corresponds with that previously mentioned, as worked upon the altar cloth of St. Sophia at Constantinople.*   The Apostles were similarly figured on the vertical band, in the centre of the back of the vestment. On this side, too, in its upper portion, worked in letters of gold and silk, was the inscription :—

✠ S. HUNGARORUM R. ET GILSA
DILECTA SIBI CONJUX
MITTUNT HÆC MUNERA DNO
APOSTOLICO IOHANNE.

"Etienne, King of Hungary, and Gisela, his dear wife, sent this present to the Apostolic Lord John."

The only Pope of the name of John, who was a contemporary of Etienne, was John XVIII., Pope from 1003 to 1009 ; this vestment, therefore, dates from the beginning of the eleventh century.

Of this period, possibly, is a Greek embroidery

* See p. 43.

preserved in the treasury of St. Peter's at Rome, and considered by connoisseurs of the present time as the most superb embroidery in the world. It is the

Fig. 32.—The Imperial Dalmatic, preserved in St. Peter's in Rome, side with the Representation of the Last Judgment.

celebrated imperial dalmatic (fig. 32). The following description of it is quoted chiefly from M. Ed. Didron's *Report upon the Decorative Arts* (1878).

The foundation of the dalmatic is of blue silk,

scattered over which are small crosses of gold and silver within circles of gold (*stauracis*). Upon the back, front, and shoulders are figured various subjects which, considered together, intensify the unity of the idea thereon expressed, viz., the glory of Jesus Christ on earth and in heaven. The Transfiguration and the Last Judgment are depicted in two large central roundels on the back and front respectively. On the shoulders are the sacraments of bread and wine. Lady Marian Alford gives a description of the embroidery thus: "It is done chiefly in gold, the draperies in basket and laid stitches; the faces in white silk split stitch, flat, with finely drawn outlines in black silk. The hair, the shadowy part of the draperies, and the clouds are worked in fine gold and silver thread, with dark outlines." To continue M. Didron's description: On the Mount of the Transfiguration (indicated by the Greek word *Metamorphose*) are green branches bearing flowers and fruit (treated in an Oriental manner), a small bird just below the figure of Christ is diapered in gold and green. The other side is, if anything, more remarkable on account of the great number of figures[*] defiling before Christ the Saviour and Judge, sitting in heaven with angels and saints on His right and left.

Greek inscriptions upon the dalmatic leave little room for doubting its Greek origin; it is called "imperial" because Charlemagne is said to have worn it "when," says Canon Rock, "he sang the Gospel at High Mass at the altar, vested as a deacon, the day

---

[*] The dresses, especially of the crowned personages, have a close resemblance to those of Justinian and the Empress Theodora, in the Ravenna Mosaics of the sixth century.

he was crowned emperor in St. Peter's, by Pope Leo III." The accuracy of this tradition, however, is much questioned. We fancy the dalmatic belongs to a less ancient period than the year 800. On examining it, we favour the opinion that it was more probably made in the eleventh or twelfth centuries for some other potentate who, according to custom, officiated as a deacon at the Mass ; in any case this magnificent vestment is not of later workmanship than that of the twelfth century.* Since that time it has been used by the deacon charged with the chanting of the Gospel in Greek at solemn festivals. The embroidery on this precious robe is a marvel of skill, such as has not been since surpassed nor probably previously equalled.

The two sides of the imperial dalmatic have been engraved and described in the *Annales archéologiques* by Didron, and in the splendid volume published by imperial authority at Vienna, entitled *Die Kleinodien des Heil.-Römischen Reiches Deutscher nation.*

Summary.—On the whole then, the antiquity of embroidery is lost in a sort of fabulous epoch, and little more than records are to be found of it. The

---

* Signor Galletti, Professor of Embroidery to the Pope, says "it is undoubtedly of the eighth century" (see *Needlework as Art*, p. 319). In this connection, too, we may revert to the mention in the *Liber Pontificalis* by Athanasius, the librarian, of the influx towards the end of the seventh century, into Rome, of Greek embroiderers, who had fled from Constantinople. It is interesting, moreover, to compare details in this dalmatic, such as the crosses (*stauracin*), especially those along the skirts, with crosses in ivory diptychs of the sixth to eighth centuries. Similar comparisons might be instituted in respect of other details too numerous to specify here.

period from Jesus Christ to the twelfth century may perhaps be regarded as its heroic epoch. Christians in the catacombs, Roman emperors of the world, Byzantines impregnated with an Oriental sense of splendour, bishops and abbots in their immense monasteries, queens and princesses in their castles and strongholds, all seem to have been equally attracted towards the art of embroidery during the first twelve hundred years of our era. Their works possess a sort of mystical solemnity of distinction. Their materials are somewhat coarse in texture, the threads rather large, and the stitches of little variety; drawing is facile in defining contours; colours are flat in tint. The simplicity of execution, marking even the most sumptuous of the embroideries then made, is a characteristic of the style of this period, which presents an unmistakable contrast with that of later centuries.

CHAPTER IV.

FROM THE CRUSADES TO THE SIXTEENTH CENTURY.

THE great events, with the effect of which Europe throbbed for more than a century, exercised a potential influence over the sumptuary arts; we allude to the Crusades.

Little by little it became a custom with the Western devotees to make pilgrimages to the Holy Land; until, in 1095, the Council of Clermont initiated a crusading movement towards the East, thus stirring European forces into an activity which for over two hundred years was ceaselessly fomented. Great bands of nobles, all clad in armour,—*fervestus*, as it was then said,—departed for Palestine; and on their return they were garbed with rich stuffs of the East, and fully impressed with the remembrance of Oriental splendours at Constantinople and towns in Asia Minor. The costumes, pouches, and caparisons which they brought back were rich in embroideries, and were beheld with admiration by the needle-workers of the West.

Pisans, Genoese, and Venetians furnished ships and armies for these distant campaigns, receiving in exchange the spoils of the vanquished Saracens.

The fourth crusade begun in 1202 under the command of Baldwin, Count of Flanders, had for its allies,

Venetians under Doge Dandolo, and seized Constantinople. The crusaders plundered the capital of its accumulations of wealth. The fêtes which followed the capture of the town completely dazzled the crusaders, and of this Robert de Clari, a companion of Villehardouin, has given an account, from which we make an extract. At the coronation of Baldwin, of which he was a witness, he says, " After the count had been accoutred in a splendid panoply,* a sumptuously embroidered mantle, jewelled with precious stones, was thrown over him; the eagles embroidered on its outside flashed so brilliantly in the sunlight that it seemed as if the mantle was a-blaze."

Mathew Paris says that at the sacking of Antioch in 1098, gold, silver, and priceless costumes were so equally distributed amongst the crusaders, that many who the night before were famishing and imploring for relief, suddenly found themselves overwhelmed with wealth.

Ancient stuffs and Byzantine embroideries, which have been there since 1204, are still to be seen in the treasury of Halberstadt, in Westphalia. They most probably came from Constantinople, which was spoiled in that year.

The thirteenth century is certainly conspicuous for an increased demand in the West for embroideries. Many crusaders made offerings to churches of plunder from Palestine. St. Louis, on his return from the first crusade, offered thanks at St. Denis to God for mercies bestowed on him during his six years' absence and

---

* See *L'Ornement dans les Tissus*, by Dupont-Auberville and V. Gay, p. 20.

travel, and presented some richly embroidered stuffs to be used on great occasions as coverings to the reliquaries containing the relics of holy martyrs. .

At this time stuffs and embroideries were used for decorating everything almost. Not only were walls hung with them, and priests clad in them, but statues of saints were also bedecked with them, and altars were inclosed within hangings, like curtains which could be drawn and thrown back at will. These altar hangings were generally embroidered with the figures of the saints to whom the altars were dedicated. Further than this, wardrobes and cupboards were adorned with stuffs on which heraldic bearings were blazoned with the utmost art of the needle-worker.

Under Louis the Young, and since 1147, the heraldic shield of France had been powdered with *fleurs de lys*. Charles V., however, reduced the number of these emblems to three, in honour of the Holy Trinity. Following royal example, every knight displayed his own particular colours at tournaments, and on military service; and the right of appropriating to itself a distinctive blazon or coat of arms was granted to every noble family.

These heraldic badges, as a rule, were of complicated forms, and exacted a high degree of skill from the embroideresses who had to work them. Fresh varieties of stitch consequently were invented. *Opus plumarium*, or feather stitch, and *opus pulvinarium*, a term somewhat loosely applied to embroidering, diaperings, or powderings of small devices, whence *sablé*, scatterings like gravel, *damier* or chequers, *ondé* or waved, *damassé* or damasked, were extensively used in embroideries on chests.   Besides these, there was the *opus consutum*, or work made with bits of stuff, either sewn together as in patchwork, or sewn one on to the other as in *appliqué* embroidery.   The separate bits were often embroidered by themselves; they were then placed upon the material selected and edged round with gold cord.   The applications   (*appliqués*) were as a rule sewn, though sometimes it was thought sufficient to   stick them merely to their foundation grounds.   Thus in the inventory of Philip the Good we find the entry of a cope of white   damask   cloth, powdered over with angels in gold embroidery, fixed with glue only upon the aforesaid cope.

Fig. 33.—Italian embroidery of the thirteenth century.

From this time forward *appliqué* embroideries (*i.e.*, composed of pieces separately   worked   and   then fastened to a foundation, thereby giving a character of slight relief to the complete work) have played an important part. Figures were frequently embroidered upon the fabric of the ground, such as velvet or cloth of gold;

but the heads to them would be wrought separately, and upon a stuff of different texture, such as satin. To the present day this class of embroidery is successfully produced.

Now, without desiring to depreciate the unquestionable merit belonging to many specimens of this *appliqué* class, we cannot withhold the expression of an opinion that it has an inherent defect in detracting from unity of work. The quality of unity in works of art, which gives the impression not only of the influence of a single source of inspiration and sentiment, directing the dexterity of the hand in wielding brush, graver, or needle—this quality is too precious to be subjected to risks to which simplifications, for the sake of rapidity in execution, are almost certain to expose it. Whenever as good effects as are obtainable in *applique* embroidery can be secured without having recourse to this particular method, it is preferable not to use it ; the chances of diminishing the suppleness of an embroidery are thereby avoided, and rigid forms, with a tendency to incongruous exaggeration in relief effects, are far less likely to manifest themselves. Faults like these are too frequently met with in *appliqués* embroideries.

Arms on banners, and oriflammes fluttering in the wind, had to be seen on both sides of the material into which they were embroidered. A sense of this condition led to the adoption of a method of needlework which, according to the apt expression of the times " *à deux endroiz*," was equally well carried out on the back and front of a stuff.

The use of Arabic inscriptions upon phylacteries and cognate decorative bands for costumes arose in embroi-

deries of the Crusading periods ; and was substituted for
that of Roman characters upon scrolls and labels such
as are to be seen wrought in Middle Age tapestries to
explain the names and actions of the figures thereon
depicted.

Towards the end of St. Louis' reign (1270) textile
stuffs were employed for book covers.* Silks, velvets,
satins, and damasks, covered with little flowers embroidered in gold and with pearls, were so used. The
library of Jean Duc de Berry, which has been described
by Douet d'Arcq, contained books of Hours, Bibles, and
Psalters, bound in ruby coloured or purple velvets,
tawny satins, fair blue silks or cloths of gold " wrought
with *fleurs de lys*, birds, and images." Leaves, flowers,
and figures of men and animals were traced in threads
of gold or silver upon a great variety of tissues. Pearls
and coral even, introduced into them, enriched the
effect of these patiently produced works.

The book of crafts by Etienne Boileau, provost of
the merchants in 1258 to 1268, contains a curious
enumeration of the different craft guilds of Paris.

Amongst those allied with our subject we find—

"Spinners of silk using large and small spindles."

" Makers of thread and silk fringes for the coifs of
ladies, pillow cases, and the hangings (or baldachinos)
over altars, which were made with the needle or in
frames."

" Makers of Paris cloth of silk, velvets, and *bourserie
en lac*."

" The tapicers, or makers of the *tapis sarrasinois* (or
Saracen cloths), who say that their craft is for the

* *Les Manuscrits*, by De Lecoy de la Marche, p. 344.

service only of churches, or great men like kings and counts."

And finally, "embroiderers and embroideresses": many of these embroideresses were skilful in draughts-manship; as, for instance, Dame Margot and Dame Aalès, of whom the additional record states that both were "illuminators." A member of the guild was pro-hibited from using gold of less value than "eight sous, (about 6s.) the skein; he was bound to use the best silk, and never to mix thread with silk because that made the work false and bad." This guild of em-broideresses was incorporated under the title of "St. Clare." Up to the last century its two sections were respectively named "freed workers" and "frogs," the latter quaint denomination applying to the less skilful workers who could never aspire to be "free," and who it was said never drank anything but water. The test or trial piece, prescribed for a worker who was the son of a master embroiderer, was "a single figure, a sixth of natural size, to be shaded in gold." Whilst one, not the son of a master embroiderer, would be required to produce "a complete incident with many figures." The book of crafts also classes "cutters-out and stencillers" amongst workmen employed in the in-dustry of embroidery, as well as "chasuble-makers, and makers of Saracenic alms-bags (*aumônières sarrasinoises*).

The wearing of these pouches or purses, pendent from girdles or belts, came into fashion during the Crusades. Money, papers, prayer-books, and gloves were carried in them. They were almost always beautifully embroidered, generally with coats of arms.

" Margaret the emblazoner " is specified in the list of freed workers and makers of pouches.

One of the finest pouches known is that containing the treasures of the cathedral of Troyes; it is said to have belonged to the Count of Champagne, Thibaut IV., called the Singer (1201—1233). Upon it is figured a youthful Saracen draped in a white mantle which covers his head and shoulders, and falls over a close-fitting under-jacket, below which in ample flowing folds is a petticoat. Lower down he is represented as slaying a lion at the feet of Eleanor of Aquitain. The figures, arabesques, and leaves are embroidered with silks on linen, cut out and then applied (*appliqué*) to a crimson velvet ground.

An illustration of another and traditionally earlier pouch is given in Arnaud's book on the province of Champagne, and is reputed to have belonged to Henry the Generous, who lived from 1152 to 1181.

Upon opening the tomb of Pierre Mauclerc, Duke of Brittany (1212—1250), in the abbey of St. Yved de Braine, a very remarkable pouch was discovered, which has been drawn by Gaignères, and published by Mont-faucon. The groundwork of gold tissue is ornamented with trellis or lozenge shapes, within which are twenty-nine different blazons, that of Brittany occupying the centre. Is it possible that these give us, as it were, a list of the knights who accompanied the Duke of Brittany on his crusade to Palestine?

In the Delaherche collection are two notable alms-bags or pouches for ladies, ornamented in a most characteristic manner with embroideries of the thirteenth century. In the cut we give of one (fig. 34) a seated angel with extended wings is worked on the flap or upper portion of the bag; below are curious types of

Fig. 34.—Pouch of the thirteenth century (Delaherche collection).

the centaur species, emblems of pride and gallantry. Such figures are often depicted in the illuminations of thirteenth century MSS. as symbols of the debasement

of man to the level of brute beasts. The embroidery
upon the alms-bag under notice is done with silk and
Cyprus gold thread, and must have been highly remarkable in its pristine state; the ground of green velvet,
backed with linen, is unfortunately much worn. The
opposite side is of green flowered Lucca damask,
patterned with birds. In former times this pouch belonged to the Chatelaines of the Duchy of Bar.

Such pouches were always trimmed either with little
knobs and tassels made òf thread or metal; some were
hung with small bells, mentioned by the chronicler as
" *Ung bourselot cloqueté d'argent*" (a pouch with silver
bells).

Leather was also used for pouches, in which the
baldrick for a sword, or the harness for a horse, could
be carried.

Fashion in these things survived the times of the
Crusades, after which the warlike character of them
became modified. A pouch in the Bonnaffé collection
is of fourteenth century embroidery, decorated with the
figures from the *Romance of the Rose*, and is a very
interesting specimen. It recalls a phrase used in respect
of a band described in the inventory of Charles V. as
being decked " with trees and ladies" (fig. 35).

From the fourteenth to sixteenth centuries the city of
Caen was noted for its embroidered bags and purses,
which had the local name of "tasques,"* whence the
street inhabited by the embroiderers was called the
Rue Tasquière. They were sold all over Europe.
Jacques de Cahaignes sent one as a gift of great value
to Joseph Scaliger when he became rector of the

* From the Italian *tasca*, purse.

university of Leyden. From a book published in 1588, entitled *Recherches et Antiquités sur la ville de Caen*, by Charles de Bourgueville, Sieur de Bras, we

Fig. 35.—Pouch of French fourteenth-century work (in the Bonnaffé collection).

learn that "as for Caen pouches, none made in other towns can compare with them for choiceness, character, and exquisite materials, such as velvets of all colours,

6

gold, silver, and other threads, or in suitability for the use of nobles, justices, ladies, and maidens, so that it is a common proverb to speak of 'Caen pouches above all others.'"

Charles of Neufchatel in 1481 gave the cathedral of Besançon a mitre which had been embroidered in Caen;* the stones which enriched it have all disappeared, but the mitre still exists.

The subjects in designs at this period, especially those for orphreys and ecclesiastical ornaments, are generally panelled

Fig. 36.—Embroidery of the fifteenth century (in the Cluny Museum).

within quatre-foils (fig. 36), and similar shapes, which occur also in contemporary painted glass windows. The scenes from the life of our Saviour, embroidered on the cope of St. Maximin (Var), are framed or panelled in this manner.

Similar treatment is observable in the pourpoint of Charles of Blois, killed at the battle of Auray (1364); it is of silk embroidered with octagonal compartments alternately filled with a lion and an eagle. .

The altar-frontal in St. Martin's at Liège is perhaps one of the more beautiful of religious fourteenth-century embroideries. It measures 3 metres in length by ·18 metre wide. Different episodes, from the life

* *Sigillographie de Normandy*, by de Farcy.

of the canonized bishop of Tours, patron saint of the church, are represented in a long series; each episode being separated from its neighbour by trees or some architectural *motif*.

It is no doubt a work by one of the celebrated artists of Tours, who, like those in England of the eleventh century, were notable equally as designers or MS. illuminators and embroiderers. Indeed, whenever the brush and the needle are thus interchangeable implements, a remarkable epoch in the art of embroidery reveals itself.

An origin under such conditions may be fairly claimed for a magnificently embroidered orphrey in the Spitzer collection (fig. 37), on which we have a Jesse tree. The treatment of this, and the character of

Fig. 37.—Part of an orphrey embroidered with a Jesse tree (fourteenth century).

the figures and ornamentation, are distinctly analogous
to those seen in fine stained glass and illuminated MSS.
of the fourteenth century.   The tree in full leaf rises from

Fig. 38.—Tau-shaped orphrey of Greek embroidery, thirteenth
century (in the Hochon collection).

Abraham, an old man asleep below; between the inter-
lacements of its leading branches are King David,
Solomon, and the Virgin Mary; surmounting all is the

Crucifixion. The frequent appearance of this tree of the sacred genealogy of Jesus Christ is noticeable in embroideries, stained glass windows, wall paintings, etc., of the period, and is a religious phase of that fashion for genealogical trees to which the adoption of family coats of arms gave rise. The embroidery of the Spitzer orphrey is in silk upon satin. The satin is left for the parts which show as skin in the figures; features, eyes, hair, and beards on it being embroidered with black silk in so closely pulled stitches as to be mistaken for pen and ink lines. The background is of gold thread worked in Hungary point (*point de Hongrie*).

Italy and Spain at this time were at a height of prosperity in the manufacture of beautiful stuffs and rich embroideries. The Saracens had already introduced into Sicily the art of weaving silken and golden fabrics, an industry subsequently encouraged by King Roger II. On his return from an expedition to Greece (1145) he brought with him the most skilful weavers and embroiderers whom he had taken captive at Corinth and Argos, and established them in workshops at Palermo (fig. 38). The Sicilian brocade weavers became renowned; they also produced marvellous embroideries for door hangings and floor coverings, by using two stuffs of different colours, cutting patterns out of the one and stitching them on to the other, over-stitching the junctures with variegated threads. These were called "*draps entaillés sarracinois*" (Saracenic cut cloths).

From Sicily the manufacture of fine stuffs spread to the north of Italy, and, becoming localized, the special productions of towns like Genoa, Florence, Lucca, Milan, and Venice acquired a high reputation.

A cognate movement occurred in Spain under the influence of the Saracens and Moors. It is on record that they brought over workmen from Persia who were engaged upon the monuments erected by them in Toledo and other towns of their conquest. It is not astonishing, therefore, that at the same time Persian embroidery should penetrate as far as Andalusia. Almeria, like

Palermo, had its *Hotel des Tiraz,* which rivalled the *Hotel des Tiraz* at Bagdad. The term *tiraz* was for a long time in use in the Spanish language, and was the generic name for ornamental tissues and costumes made with them.

The Spaniards excelled in stuffs of velvet raised on satin, inwoven with strands of gold and silver. Their designs have all the boldness and Oriental character which one also finds in Cordovan

Fig. 39.—Embroidery of the fourteenth century (in the Hochon collection).

decorative leathers. The colours in both are the same; and gold is cunningly used in conjunction with sombre tones, enhancing their effects with the utmost felicity.

Sometimes, however, beaten gold, when introduced in these textiles, was made to assume the shape of small plaques or thin plates of gold, upon which would be mounted several rows of pearls. But this evident abuse of the metal in its relation with a textile could not last long; and these inappropriate golden plaques were speedily modified into spangles, those pretty little discs of gold, silver, or polished steel used in certain classes of embroidery for dainty glinting effects. The Saracens are credited with the invention of spangles; and, following their example, the Spaniards made free use of them in much of their ornamental needlework. One extremely remarkable specimen of

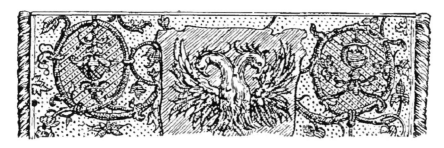

Fig. 40.—Embroidery designed by Lucas van Leyden, taken from his portrait of Maximilian I. (sixteenth century), belonging to M. Dutuit.

this spangled work is the chasuble embroidered by Isabella la Catolica, and carried by King Ferdinand to the cathedral of Granada after the taking of that town from the Moors in 1492; all the flowers upon this sumptuous vestment are worked with gold and silver spangles of different sizes indented at their centres (fig. 40).

A slightly later Spanish cope of the same characteristic work has recently been added to the Spitzer collection. Standing figures of saints under architectural canopies are embroidered upon its red velvet orphreys. The figures are in high relief of quite unusual character, and although resplendent by reason of an infinity of little golden rings instead of spangles stitched over them, their general effect is heavy. The main ground. of the chasuble is of cloth of gold; scattered in a sort of diapering pattern all over it are escutcheons bearing the Spanish arms.

The use of spangles in the French court is recorded in the royal accounts for the year 1389, where we have an entry of "iij marcs xvijs esterlins of fine gold at xxij carats, delivered to Estienne d'Epernon, gold beater, to be flattened and shaped into broom blossoms (*fleurs de genestes*), for stitching on to the two embroidered doublets of the king." *

In 1411 a pair of cuffs or sleeves made for the Duke of Burgundy were covered over with "seven thousand five hundred little twists of silver, and alternated with two thousand little scrolls of gold, the whole of them weighing twelve marcs."

At this period pearls were even more fashionable than spangles. A single instance, to show this, is worth quoting. In 1414 Charles of Orleans spent two hundred and seventy-six livres (about £40) for nine hundred and sixty pearls, which were to be used in ornamenting a great coat, on the sleeves of which were embroidered the verses of a song beginning with " Madame, I am all joyous." . . . The musical accompaniment of the words was also embroidered, the staves being worked in gold thread, and each note (of square shapes in those days) formed with four pearls.† The motive of this pattern was clearly more

---

* F. Michel, *Recherches sur les Étoffes de Soie.* According to Doursther a *marc* = 8 ounces = 64 *gros* = 160 *esterlins* = 320 *mailles* = 640 *felins.* The *marc* of Paris and Lyons = 3,777·5 English grains, or 244·75 French *grammes.*

† Quicherat, *Histoire du Costume*, p. 254.

whimsical and extravagant than likely to lead to good artistic result.

In the time of Philippe le Bel embroideries superseded furs, which, for longer than the previous century, had been the fashionable trimmings for court costumes. Philippe, who had a mania for attempting to regulate and control everything, issued in 1294 an ordinance that sanctioned the wearing of embroideries by princes of the blood royal only; but this law soon came to be more honoured in the breach than in the observance, as all who could afford it followed the fashion of the princes.

Besides for costume, embroidery was used for articles of furniture. Ornamental textiles generally were then more widely employed than nowadays.

The interior of great castles in the Middle Ages were far less divided up by such partitions as are so freely used in modern dwellings; the halls and saloons were vast, almost without decoration, and they were made habitable for the great and luxurious by hanging stuffs upon the walls, and stretching them across cords, arranged so as to subdivide the halls into compartments, bays, and recesses. Kings and princes made use of various draperies and hangings suitable to the season of the year. The chambers of the king would be called the Easter, the All Saints, or the Christmas rooms. Or, again, they would be designated after the ornament or pattern of the hangings; thus, there would be the room of the Crosses, of the Lions, etc. The stuffs for a room were of two classes—tapestry-hangings and furniture-coverings. The coverings (*courte pointeries*) included draperies for the bed. The couches or feather beds, the mattresses, and other articles were almost always bedecked with embroidered counterpanes, bed canopies, and curtains, and covers for head boards. Against one of the walls of the chamber the bed would be set, covered over with a quilt, and backed by a head board, from which was an overhanging tester with three curtains. Close at hand was a smaller overhanging canopy with draperies, behind which the king dressed.* All the hangings were embroidered with heraldic devices.

In King Charles V.'s inventory, quoted by Labarthe and given also in the *Documents pour servir à l'histoire de France*, we find many descriptions of fittings, etc., similar to those just named. As, for instance, " a chamber hung with cloth of gold, on which is a bright red velvet cross embroidered with coats of arms." " Item: a chamber hung with cloth of silver ornamented with five compass devices embroidered with the arms of France and the Dauphin; also a canopy or tester hanging, draperies for head board, and counterpane or coverlet, and three curtains of Indian cendal.

" Item : a tent of French embroidery in which are depicted the four evangelists, in a framework of arch shapes, with curtains striped in green and purple, and rayed with gold."

Kings' journeys then were not as simply conducted as now ; their luggage always included a large quantity of furniture, etc., without which they would have been unable to live in the castles where they happened to stop. It was not a question of taking clothing only, beds, linen, and draperies had to go as well. The preparations for Phillippe le Long's coronation in 1317

* *Le Meuble*, by de Champeaux, p. 75.

involved the provision of numberless chests and coffers, one of which, a large one, was for " the robes of our sire the King," * and four others " for the bed and commodities of the King." Queen Joan of Burgundy had twelve great trunks, two for her bed, six for her wardrobe, two for her ladies-in-waiting, etc. The room prepared for her majesty's use in the palace at Rheims, during her sojourn for the coronation festivities, was embroidered with " thirteen hundred and twenty-one *papegauts* (parrots) made in broidery, and blazoned with the King's arms and five hundred and sixty-one butterflies, whose wings were similarly ornamented with the Queen's arms, the whole worked in fine gold."

England whose brilliant reputation for embroideries has been already mentioned, possesses an authentic work of the fourteenth century of the highest interest, proving that she had in no way declined in the art.†
This is a pall or mortuary cloth which belongs to the Fishmongers' Company, and is traditionally said to have been used at the funeral of Sir William Walworth during the reign of Richard II., 1381. It is of long rectangular shape, with two long and two short pendent

* *Le Meuble*, by de Champeaux, p. 66.

† This fine embroidery is described at p. 262 of the Catalogue of the Special Exhibition of Works of Art, South Kensington Museum, 1862. Monsieur Biais, whose description of it Monsieur Lefebure has adopted, appears to have been misled, for the arms worked on this pall are those of the Stock-fishmongers and Salt-fishmongers united into one shield, having as supporters a merman clad in golden armour, and a mermaid with a jewel hanging from her neck, and in her hand a looking-glass. The two companies were united in 1536. The embroidery is therefore of the time of Henry VIII. Thus it supports Monsieur Lefebure's assertion in favour of England's celebrity for embroidery, and extends its application to a period a hundred and fifty years longer than he contemplates.

panels which form its border. The main ground of the pall is of fine Flemish red gold brocade. The two short pendant panels are onamented with English embroideries of St. Peter robed and seated as a pope holding the keys of Paradise* (fig. 41). Each of the two long pendant panels has in its centre Christ entrusting the keys to St. Peter, flanked by the arms and supporters of the Stock and Salt-Fishmongers' Companies united. The figures are worked in silk and gold thread couchings. The whole is remarkable for masterly design and admirable execution.

Flanders was equally celebrated for embroideries made from the drawings of artists. Many Flemish orphreys closely resemble the painted wooden triptychs of the Gothic period, which abound in the churches and museums of Belgium. Others again have all the character of old ecclesiastical stained glass windows.

The finest set of sacerdotal robes of this style is to be seen in the Ambras collection at Vienna. It consists of a chasuble, two dalmatics, three copes, and two ante pendiums. The figures upon them are embroidered in silks of many colours upon cloth of gold, from designs by the brothers Van Eyck or their pupils. Pearls surround the saints, whose crowns and *nimbi* glisten with precious stones. It is said that these magnificent vestments were used at the first chapter of the Golden Fleece held by Philip the Good on the 10th January, 1430.†

The sumptuous embroideries which belonged to Charles the Bold, son of Philip the Good, may no

---

* M. Biais, *Les Broderies anciennes à l'Exposition de Londres.*

† *Élements d'Archéologie*, by Reusens, vol. ii., p. 475.

Fig. 41.—English embroidery of the sixteenth century upon the Fishmongers' Mortuary Cloth or Pall.

doubt be attributed to Flemish art. They were taken

by the Swiss on the 3rd March, 1476, at the battle
of Gransons, in regard to which Philip de Comines
writes, "they seized his camp and cannon, and all
the tents and pavilions belonging to him and his retinue
which was very numerous, and took possession of all
the belongings of the said duke."

Du Sommerard has published the more notable of
the stuffs and embroidered standards captured at this
victory, and now preserved at Berne ; some in the
cathedral, others in the museum. Amongst the "four
hundred pieces of silk, velvet, and tapestries" is to
be found the Duke of Burgundy's yellow velvet hat,
with a diamond *porte aigrette*, whence sprang a sheaf
of plumes and pearls. The larger of the diamonds
was the famous Sancy diamond, "the largest in
Christendom," says Comines, and quoted at the present
day as one of the most exquisite jewels ever known.

Flanders and Burgundy were for so long united
under the same sovereignty that an uncertainty ob-
tains in assigning the precise origin of many stuffs
known as Burgundian in which Flemish traits frequently display themselves.

In Germany a class of work had long been produced
under the name of *opus Coloniensis* (Cologne work), in
which both weaving and embroidery were frequently
combined.

Narrow bands and braids were made in small portable low-warp frames.* Broader pieces, and involving
more intricate work, as those for orphreys on copes and

---

* These little weaving frames, adapted to either shuttle-weaving or
tapestry-weaving, are often engraved as frontispieces to pattern books
which are subsequently mentioned in the section of Laces.

chasubles, would be made in high-warp frames; that is, in frames with vertical ranks of warp as distinct from those with low or horizontal ranks of warp. Between these warps shuttles charged with various coloured threads would be thrown by the worker, who would vary the use of the shuttle with that of the needle as occasion might arise for giving increased solidity to certain details in the fabric. This varied method of execution resulted in the production of works having unmistakable characteristics; and although this combined weaving and embroidery was considerably made along the banks of the Rhine during the fifteenth and sixteenth centuries, it has since disappeared. In such small frames as those just alluded to, tapestries were produced of the character described by M. Eugene Muntz, when he writes, "It was in convents, and sometimes in castles, that hangings of small dimensions were woven, a great number of which are to be seen in the museums at Munich and Nuremberg." The South Kensington and the Cluny Museums and many well-known Parisian collections contain similar specimens. A figure, for instance, would be entirely woven; but if it were that of a bishop or king the mitre or the crown would be embroidered, and a happy effect of slight relief would be thereby secured. The engraving (fig. 43) is of a band in the South Kensington Museum. It was probably used for an altar of the Virgin, since the words "Ave Maria" and the figure of the Virgin are conspicuous amongst other figures and inscriptions in it. The heads of the figures and the objects they hold in their hands are of embroidery, the remaining parts being woven.

The design on a chasuble cross in the Hochon
collection (fig. 42) is dignified in its simplicity.   No
useless accessory detracts from the value of the woven

Fig. 42.—German embroidery (? Cologne) of the fifteenth century
(in the Hochon collection).

cloth of gold foundation in its relation to the personages
and inscriptions wrought upon it.   The heads are of
appliqué work.   In the centre is Christ on the cross;
the wounds in His body and the drops of blood from
them are embroidered in red silk; at His feet is the

sorrowing Virgin supported by St. John. Above them are the spear and the reed with sponge soaked in vinegar. Above the cross is the inscription *Pater in manus tuas.* At the lower extremity of the central limb of the cross (not shown in the cut) is a saint in armour, bearing a standard or pennon and a shield, each of these charged with nine bezants. Below is the name of the donor, Johan van Querroide.

A beautiful orphrey of similar style, belonging to Comte Charles Lair, is dated " Colonia, 1510."

Articles of costume, such as head-dresses, shoes, and

Fig. 43.—Orphrey of embroidered woven work, Cologne work (in the South Kensington Museum).

gloves have frequently been splendidly embroidered. A single chapter would not suffice to do justice to the mitres worn in old times by bishops and abbots of monasteries. Their shape was modified, and became larger from century to century. Up to the twelfth century they were small and low; as they increased in height in the thirteenth and fourteenth centuries, so the angles in them became more acute. In the fifteenth century were developed the high and curved shapes which mitres retain to the present day.

7

A fine fifteenth-century mitre, remarkable for the figures embroidered on it, is preserved in St. Gildas de Ruys in Morbihan.* It is .38 metre high and .30 metre wide; its two lappets are .37 metre long. The ground of this mitre is white silk, with vertical stripes of silver threads. On each of its sides are two figures, wrought on stout linen, and then applied (*appliqués*) to the silk ground. Those on the front are of two abbots, doubtless the founders of the priory; they are surrounded with stars worked in gold thread. Upon the lappets are *appliqués* figures, one a St. Sebastian pierced with arrows, the other a headless martyr at the burning stake.

The Cluny Museum possesses many remarkable mitres. The Spitzer collection contains one of German fifteenth-century work, notable as much for the fineness of its embroidery as for the goldsmith's work upon it.

And now, cursorily alluding to ecclesiastical gloves and shoes worn by prelates at great Church functions, we may briefly say, that as a rule they are examples of most finished embroidery in the rendering of the emblems and graceful interlacing scrolls which enter into the patterns wrought upon them.

In the inventories of the possessions of the Bayeux Cathedral is an entry of " two woollen mittens (*mytaines*), with embroidery, on the hands, of two figures of St. Veronica surrounded by pearls."

Ladies also wore ornamental gloves made of silken material, and embroidered in gold and silver thread.

* *Abécédaire de Caumont*, p. 729.

Of such character no doubt would be the "glove, which gold and silken broidery bore," filched from and then returned with heart-aching lamentings to his beauteous Laura by Petrarch.*

On the whole then it will have been seen that the employment of embroidery was gradually extended to all parts and articles of costume, so that it is not surprising to find that every household of any position during the fifteenth century retained the services of an embroiderer by the year.†

The preparation of colours, whether for painting or for dyeing threads and textile fabrics, was a matter which received close attention from artists of the Middle Ages. Many undertook long journeys to obtain the more famous recipes,‡ which they filed, subsequently adding to and correcting them as experience dictated. And in this direction little can be more instructive than the inquiry conducted in 1409 and 1410 by a Parisian named Jean le Bègue, clerk to the Mint, who proceeded to Italy to study processes of colour manufacture. At Bologna he happened upon a Flemish embroiderer called Thierry, who had worked for the Duke of Milan, and previously in London. This Thierry taught him many new methods in the manufacture of colours. Le Bègue wrote a full account of all he learned and noted, and his manuscript is preserved to this day.

By such gleanings and interchanges of ideas the number of tones and colours available for the use of

---

* See *Sonnets*, 166 and 168.
† Quicherat's *Histoire du Costume*, p. 279.
‡ *Les Manuscrits*, by Lecoy de La Marche, p. 306.

the embroiderer was considerably augmented. The celebrated dyer Jean Gobelin lived in the middle of the fifteenth century. His dye works and model work-rooms were erected on the banks of the Bièvre, where his descendants continued the business for two centuries; but his name is made more famous by reason of its inseparable association with the national manufactory of the Gobelins tapestries, which was in truth a development of Jean Gobelin's original workshops.

In 1462 René d'Anjou, who had been crowned King of Naples and Sicily, presented Angers Cathedral with very gorgeous ornaments at a cost of 40,000 écus. They were the works of one of the famed embroiderers of Avignon, Pierre du Vaillant by name, on whom the title of Painter to the King of Sicily was also conferred. These ornaments, dedicated to "Messire St. Maurice," the patron saint of the cathedral, consisted of a chasuble, a tunic, a dalmatic, a cope, and an altar hanging; in all, five articles, entered in the inventories of the chapter under the comprehensive title of "the Great Embroidery" (*la Grande Broderie*).* The design, displaying a history of St. Maurice, was executed upon a groundwork, dotted with blossoms. The altar frontal was of velvet "*paramentum de velosio, cum armis Domini Renati Regis Siciliæ et defunctæ Reginæ Ysabellis*," with the arms of the Sovereign Lord René, King of Sicily, and of the defunct Queen Isabella. Around these escutcheons were panels of cloth of gold "*panno aureo*," on which were emblems of the Passion, "*ad ymagines Passionis*," lozengy diaperings, "*alia cum lozangiis et corona*," and crowns, "*seminata stellis*,"

---

* *Broderies et Tissus de la Cathédrale d'Angers*, by de Farcy.

spotted with stars, "*angelis aureis quorum quidem in-censunt*," with golden angels, some of them swinging censers, "*alii portant cruces et calices*," others bearing crosses and chalices. This variety of devices conveys an impression of the splendour of this "great embroidery" which evoked great admiration during the three hundred years it was preserved as the most important ornamental work in the cathedral at Angers.

Still to be seen in the church of Naintré near Châtellerault, in Vienne, is a remarkable chasuble of corresponding date. Upon its orphrey is figured St. Thomas holding the New Testament in one hand and a spear in the other; above is an archbishop robed in chasuble, adorned with a cross, and carrying an archiepiscopal processional cross, with one cross bar. Upon the cross, embroidered at the back of the chasuble, is the Virgin seated in majesty, wearing shoes on her feet in accordance with iconographical ruling, and holding the naked infant Jesus on her lap; below are St. James the Greater and St. Barbe, who carries in his hand a tower, representative of that in which his father confined him; the whole work is finely wrought.*

Wherever a royal or princely court attracted stateliness and luxury, its influence gave impulse to the art of embroidery, as we have seen in regard to the rich surroundings of Philip the Good and Charles the Bold in Flanders.

Charles VII., having established his court at Bourges, many embroiderers came to work there, amongst whom we note Colin Jolye as the producer,

---

* See *Broderies et Tissus*, by M. L. de Farcy.

in 1454, of a splendid cope ordered by the king, and
of which a description is given in the *Bulletin Archéologique* (vol. iii., p. 86).   Simonne de Gaules was
another equally distinguished needle-worker at Bourges.

Louis XI. was deeply interested in the industry
of his kingdom.   From Orleans he issued, 23rd
November, 1466, letters patent to establish a manufacture of silken cloths in the town of Lyons, "in which,
it is said, the industry has already been begun."
Shortly after, he took up his residence at Tours, and
watched with close interest the embroiderers at work,
of whom Jéhan de Moucy was the best known.   His
Majesty determined to associate silk-weavers with them,
and accordingly had artisans brought over from Italy
in 1470, amongst whom were "a silk-trimmer, a dyer,
a thread-spinner, and a gold thread-drawer."   The
chief of this body of artificers was François le Calabrais.
Mulberry trees were planted and cultivated, and weaving
frames set up; the *Gros de Tours* became celebrated,
and in 1546 a Venetian ambassador reports finding
eight thousand frames weaving silks in Touraine.

For many years, and after Gregory X. had made it
the residence of the popes, and had imported workers
from Sicily, Naples, and Lucca (1309—1377), Avignon
was noted for its chasuble embroiderers' workrooms.
Pierre du Vaillant, the maker of the "great embroideries"
for Angers Cathedral, already mentioned, hailed from
Avignon.

Nismes adopted the arts of making silk stuffs from
Avignon, and has ever since been an important centre
for them.

In 1494 King Charles VIII., like René of Anjou,

returned victorious from an expedition into Sicily and the kingdom of Naples, bringing with him great wealth in the shape of objects of art and valuable textiles, and surrounded himself with Italian artists who resided close to his palace, the Chateau d'Amboise, where he and his wife, Anne of Brittany, lived (fig. 44). Philip de Comines mentions " the many workmen excelling in divers crafts," whom the king " brought back from Naples." They were placed under the direction of Panthaléon Conte and his wife, whose wages amounted to twenty Tournese pounds, or nearly £4 a month.*

From this time may be said to have commenced the growth in France of Italian influence, which developed itself throughout the whole of the sixteenth century.

Italy had become the seat of a luxury unknown to any other country, since the splendours of Byzantium seven or eight centuries previously.

The Medici lived in a magnificence and pomp of which we can form some conception from contemporary paintings. Benozzo Gozzoli's fresco in the Riccardi Palace at Florence presents us with a portrait of Lorenzo dei Medici on horseback, in the character of one of the Magian kings bringing gifts, and it is difficult to know which most to admire, the sumptuous and glittering embroideries with which his costume is decorated, or the rich and elegant trappings of his white steed.

With the Medicean period we enter upon an epoch of the Renaissance, the glory of which culminated in the sixteenth century. But before leaving the Middle Ages we must refer to the charm of their art. If less studied in the refinement of its productions than that

* *Archives de l'Art Français*, by A. de Montaiglon.

of a subsequent and dazzling age, it was nevertheless inspired with truer sentiment and purer taste, as may have been inferred from our sketch of embroidery done from the twelfth to the sixteenth century.

Fig. 44.—Coloured embroidery, with the cypher of Anne of Brittany (in the Hochon collection).

Summary.—Stuffs upon which embroidery was worked in the Middle Ages were called by various names, such as linen cloths, cloth of gold and of silver, baudekin, samit, cendal (often mentioned as Indian cendal), velvet, camoca, and tiraz or silk weavings, etc. Many long dissertations have been written by different persons as to the technical nature of the stuffs so named; Francisque Michel, in his *Recherches sur les Étoffes de Soie*, has nearly exhausted the subject,* dealing with it in a masterly manner. Those who desire to identify the various methods of producing textile fabrics will find in Monsieur Michel's and Dr. Rock's learned books material and guidance for their studies. We of course cannot here propose to do more than discuss ornamental embroidery; and in this respect we may

* See also *Textile Fabrics*, by the Very Rev. Daniel Rock, D.D.

broadly say that the unaffectedness of design which marked the immediately preceding period is less conspicuous in work of the Middle Ages. One perceives that the extension of Oriental and Byzantine influence, aided by the crusades, helped both designer and embroiderer to step as it were on to a new stage.

Hence their work is more varied in execution, stiches are better selected and applied, colouring is richer, and shapes of forms are rendered with less restraint; the whole effect is still characterized by sincerity and frankness in inspiration and execution.

Fig. 45.—Italian embroidery, fifteenth century (in the Hcchon collection).

Heraldic and religious subjects almost equally engaged the needle of the embroiderer, a preference being shown for saints with militant attributes. And it seems as though religious art in its expressions in churches and monasteries was imbued with the spirit animating the crusaders on their way to Jerusalem. St. Maurice, centurion of Roman phalanxes; St. Martin, who was a soldier before he was consecrated bishop ; St. George represented as " a knight on horse-back killing a wild beast " (*ung chevalier à cheval qui occit un beste*), and above all, St. Michael piercing with his lance the devil beneath his feet—the famous saint invoked by pious pilgrims at his shrine on the "mount exposed to the buffetings of the waves,"—all these saints are those whose effigies embroiderers from the twelfth to fifteenth centuries preferred to depict. Saints wearing armour were thus favourite subjects ; and this militaryism is more or less distinctive of embroideries at this period.

When our Saviour was represented it would be as Christ crucified, surrounded by soldiers nailing Him to the cross, or throwing dice for His garments ; or else as Christ issuing from the tomb (*issant d'ung tumbel*), to the amazement of the soldiery set to guard it.

Four ecclesiastical ornaments, sent as a gift to the King of England, his son-in-law, were chosen by Charles VI. for their embroideries of "the Blessed Trinity, the Mount Olivet, St. Michael and St. George."

We have mentioned the importance assigned to the display of heraldic bearings and pennons by knights on going into battle or taking part in tournaments. Princesses presided as umpires over these latter, which were held in the lists ; and when applying themselves to make embroideries for a church of either "our Lady enthroned " or "a coronation of our Lady in the midst of angels," they would introduce their own portraits into them.

Thus, then, religious and heraldic subjects give the peculiar characteristic observable in artistic needle-work of the Middle Ages. It is one which does not similarly reveal itself in works of a later time when customs more pacific and manners less severe prevailed. At the commencement of the new period there was doubtless a tendency towards refining and perfecting methods of execution, in the results of which, however, we may look in vain for that noble boldness and loyal frankness of style which pervaded the arts of the Middle Ages.

CHAPTER V.

FROM THE SIXTEENTH CENTURY TO THE DEATH OF
LOUIS XIV.

LIKE other arts, embroidery in France and elsewhere
during the sixteenth century was dominated by Italian
influence.

Italy, of all countries that were engaged in weaving
industries, was the most proficient; from Sicily to
Genoa, Milan and Venice, every town more or less had
its workrooms for weaving flax, cotton, and especially
silk.

Genoa and Venice were the principal European ports
for trade in silks from the Levant. Both in Sicily and
Lombardy silk-worm nurseries (*magnaneries*) were
started, and sericulture was successfully pursued.
Lucca gold threads rivalled those of Cyprus, whilst
Milanese needles were reckoned as good as those
from Damascus. Circumstances therefore concurred
in making Italy a principal centre for beautiful
textiles.

The court of the popes, at the times of such pontiffs
as Julius II. de la Rovere, Leo X. dei Medici, and
Paul III. dei Farnesi, became the rallying point of the
best artists and handicraftsmen. And at the hands of
the popes, the Venetian doges, and dukes of Florence,

Milan, and Ferrara, there was no lack of constant orders for important works, which kept the Italian embroiderers unceasingly employed.

The execution was carried to a very high degree of finish. The smallest details were solicitously cared for by the embroiderers, and the perfection of work complied with the exactions of consumers possessing a love for artistic productions. The flat tints of the Middle Ages were wholly inadequate for embroideries, which were required to be as subtle as paintings in delicate tones and imperceptible blendings of colours. Gradation of colours for threads, etc., was carried as far as possible, split stitches of minute size were employed for rendering with artful effect undulating contours and skin textures in figure subjects, and these were carried to exaggeration, when with questionable propriety embroiderers called in the aid of the paint brush to second the work of their needles.

Variety in embroideries was inexhaustible. Venetians, noted for skill in glass-work of all sorts, embroidered with coloured glass beads, much in the manner of the ancient Egyptians.* To some extent these bead embroideries may be likened to mosaics made with little tesseræ. At the South Kensington Museum some few remarkable specimens are to be seen† (fig. 46). But they are scarcely commendable from the artistic point of view, notwithstanding a certain gayness of effect in them. A few little beads and pearls can no doubt be happily introduced into certain portions of embroideries, whereas work ex-

* See Egyptian bead work in the Louvre and British Museum.
† These are considered to be of late twelfth-century work.

clusively done with them is usually unworthy of consideration from any high standpoint of criticism.*
Their weight loads the stuff on to which they are

worked, and necessarily gives it a disagreeable rigidity. The least accident almost may break the thread holding them, with the result that they fall off and leave bare spaces in the embroidery. Any analogy this beadwork may have with mosaic inlaying enforces the reservation of anything in the nature of mosaic work to its special purpose in connection with architecture, and demonstrates also that the flexible nature of a textile is incompatible with any modification of a decorative process thoroughly suited to flat, rigid, wall surfaces.

From one end of Europe to the other Italian styles of embroidery were more or less imitated.

Fig. 46.—Venetian bead embroidery of the twelfth century (?) (in the Kensington Museum).

In 1551 the Parisian Corporation of Embroiderers issued a notice that, "for the future the colouring in representations of nude figures and faces should be done in three or four gradations

* It certainly recalls the wampum or belts and moccasins of North Americans.

of carnation dyed silk, and not as formerly with white silks." *

Artists of distinction were not above making and supplying designs for embroidery. Vasari relates that Perino del Vaga made drawings of eight subjects from the life of St. Peter for embroideries upon a cope for Pope Paul VIII.

Raphael himself paid some attention to designs for embroidery, and in Paris is a specimen worked from a design which he made in compliance with an order from Francis I. It is an oval medallion preserved in the Cluny Museum (fig. 47). Originally it was part of a set of furniture embroideries done upon a golden ground, which consisted of coverings and hangings for a bed, four arm-chairs, eighteen folding-stools, a table-cover, a fire-screen, and a canopy for "the coronation chamber." This chamber was decorated with forty subjects, representing episodes in the history of the Jews, and set within panels or cartouches, surrounded by many figures. These magnificent embroideries were in later years given to the abbey of St. Denis, where they were kept until the Revolution. Then, alas! they were destroyed, and nought remains of them but the solitary fragment in the Cluny Museum. This measures .80 metre in width and .50 metre in height. Upon it is depicted the scene of the Israelites dancing in a plain round the golden calf, which surmounts a silver column. In the background to the left is Moses receiving the tables of the Law; on the right are the Israelitish tents. The action of the figures

* Victor Gay, *Glossaire Archéologique*, p. 227.

is pourtrayed with great grace, whilst the whole

Fig. 47.——"Dance round the Golden Calf." An oval panel ot embroidery after a design by Raphael (in the Cluny Museum).

composition reflects a masterly execution. It is much to be regretted that this embroidery of first-class historical importance is in a bad state of preservation. A book published in Paris in 1775, entitled the *Richesses Tirées du Trésor de l'Abbaye de Saint Denis*, contains a complete description of "the Coronation Chamber," with its forty medallions of embroidery.*

Many French inventories include mentions of "embroidered pictures." In that of Charles V. there is one of "a picture of embroidery, with a portrait of *Monseigneur le Dauphin* mounted on a black horse, driving it with a stick which he holds in his hand."

Margaret of Austria owned several portable embroidered pictures. One of a pair is described as a "broidery, in which are Our Lady, St. Catherine, and St. John the Evangelist, fitted into a scarlet velvet case."

When the Augustinian friars came in 1659 and took up their abode at the convent of Brou, they made an inventory of the things they found there, amongst which were "two pictures of needlework done by the very hand of the foundress, one representing the entombment of our Lord, the other the Presentation in the Temple."

Soon pictures of this class were made of a larger size than previously. Monsieur Léon de Laborde writes: "The art of embroidery then became a serious and esteemed sister of painting; for the needle, in truth a painter's brush, traversed its canvas, leaving behind it a dyed thread as a colour, producing a painting soft in tone, ingenious in touch—a picture without glistening surface, brilliant without harshness."

* Léon de Laborde, *La Renaissance des Arts à la Cour de France*, vol. i., p. 993.

In the Spitzer collection we find one of such pictures, most curious as an historical scene of manners and customs (fig. 49). In the yard of one of his palaces is Henry II., with Diane de Poitiers and numerous courtiers, looking on at a fight between dogs and a bear. The energy of the dogs and the keen interest of the spectators are admirably interpreted. Moved to pity by the sad plight of one of the dogs, which is covered with gore from the savage wounds of the bear, Diane is directing an attendant to stay the fight.

Fig. 48.—Panel or cartouche of Italian embroidery of the sixteenth century.

All the figures of the persons are excellently rendered, particularly that of the king. The stitches in silks used to depict his face are minute, and so ably disposed as to give a most lifelike appearance to the king's countenance.

The animals are treated with greater breadth of execution, and this is increased to give due imitative effect to the textures of the ground and of the masonry of the castle about it. This is a very fine work of French art.

We can safely say as much of another picture in the same collection, the principal composition in which represents the Entombment of our Lord, and might possibly have belonged formerly to the Augustinians at the Convent of Brou. Beneath this foremost scene

Fig. 49.—Bear fighting with dogs before Henry II. and Diane de Poitiers.

are compartments displaying Hell, where Jesus is seeking the prophets and saints of the old dispensation to bring them into the Kingdom of the Elect; all of which is interpreted with a really remarkable purity and vigour of drawing and needlework.

But the needle has even surpassed itself in the marvellous execution of its work for two panels, adapted for a lectern cover. The more interesting

Fig. 50.—Panel, displaying a sacramental procession, of Italian sixteenth-century embroidery.

of these shows a symbolical procession of the Holy Sacrament, in which both Old and New Testaments are typified (fig. 50). At the head of the procession is King David, dancing and singing psalms as he plays his harp. Four monks vested in copes, whose gestures are most naturally given, form the central group, carrying the Holy Sacrament upon a brancard, overshadowed by an elegant, golden, canopied shrine; behind comes, in sixteenth-century costumes, a troop of priests,

nobles, magistrates, and common folk, amongst whom
may be descried a negro. A woman wearing a crown
is seated at a window, expressing by signs her admiration. The style of the figures, and beautiful drawing
of the different facial expressions, together with the
masterly treatment of the perspective of the buildings and monuments, recall the manner of Paul
Veronese. Carried to such a pitch of perfection,
embroidery certainly attains to the charm of distinctive and unapproachable individuality. Executed
with a freedom not possible in tapestry-weaving, it
has quality of greater brilliancy than painting, and
the texture of its silks secures a play of light which
cannot be as well obtained by other means. For
subjects of small dimensions requiring close inspection,
embroidery, when of such perfection as that of this
panel, is *sui generis* and absolutely unrivalled.

The Museum of Art and Industry at Lyons contains
a picture of great beauty, representing an *Ecce Homo*,
of which we give an illustration. It is in the style
of Rembrandt's school (fig. 51).

At South Kensington is a picture, or small panel,
probably from an orphrey, of a saint seated beneath
a circular-headed niche, holding a cross and reading
the Gospels, embroidered after a design by the Floren-
tine Raffaellino del Garbo, pupil and friend of Philippo
Lippi.

But besides pictures we find at South Kensington
a series of embroidered specimens all worthy of close
study. In them, indeed, we have an incomparable
collection of works fully setting forth the history
of the art of embroidery. Let us now, however,

merely pause to examine a bewitching specimen of sixteenth-century embroidery, the design of which might almost have been inspired by Virgil's *Georgics*. The embroidery covers the outside of a casket, or coffer, fourteen and three-quarter inches long by six and a quarter high, and is evidently of French work under Italian influence. The various subjects, each

of which is emblematical of a month, are twelve in number. Four occur on the lid, namely, those applicable to September, October, November, and December. The two long panels, one at each end of the coffer, represent April, in the episode of a noble receiving a flower from a draped maiden, and August

Fig. 51.—*Ecce Homo* (an embroidered picture in the Museum of Art and Industry at Lyons).

in the harvest scene of a reaper cutting a rich field of golden wheat ; the back and front sides of the coffer are each split up into three panels, for the months of January, February, March, and May, June, July. The French inscriptions of these latter months—*Mai, Jun, Julet*—are legible ; the other months are identifiable by the zodiacal signs, one in each panel. The embroidery, which is padded, to give relief effects in various parts, such as the architectural ornaments, is worked with gold threads, whipped round with fine coloured silks ; certain forms are defined by gold cords stitched down to outline them ; the faces of the figures, and some of the charming glimpses of land-scape, are wrought in long and short stitches with coloured silks.*

Spanish embroiderers were almost equally skilful in this class of work, and did not fail to adopt many refinements of the art from the Italians. Although the execution of the Spanish work was less compact than that of the Italian, certain samples of it are hardly of inferior artistic quality ; this is specially the case with embroideries which owe both charm and style to having been made from paintings by Murillo, the master above others of the Spanish school. Of such, the Spitzer collection contains a remarkable specimen, —an embroidered picture of a holy family seated beneath a spreading tree in the midst of a sunny landscape.

Some of the Spanish embroidered pictures are worked with as sharp and crisp a relief as can be obtained in wood-carving ; as, for instance, are Adam and Eve in the Cluny Museum, a monument of deplorable taste which is in no way qualified by the surprising skill in the execution of the reliefs.

Apart from pictures, and of a broader and more decorative class, are certain very striking Spanish altar-cloths of red velvet with arabesques, having the

---

* See description of this, pp. 285, 286, *Descriptive Catalogue of the Collections of Tapestry and Embroidery in the South Kensington Museum.*

appearance of being cut or chiselled out of solid gold;
one similar to fig. 52, but with heraldic shields, has
been frequently engraved, notably in an interesting
report by Gaston le Breton upon the exhibition of

Fig. 52.—Altar frontal of velvet with Spanish embroidery of the
sixteenth century.

textiles held under the auspices of the *Union Centrale
des Arts Decoratifs.**

One of the finest sets of embroidery exhibited in the
Ancient Art Section of the Paris Universal Exhibition
of 1878 consisted of four pieces of Spanish work for

* *Les Arts du Bois, des Tissus et du Papier*, p. 173 (published by
Quantin).

funeral ceremonies (figs. 53 and 54). Square panels containing cartouches, in which were skulls, with balanced arrangements of floriated scrolls about them, formed the principal decorative *motifs* of these embroideries. The play of the elegant golden scrolls was in happy contrast with the sombre objects within the cartouches, and is likened by M. Théodore Biais, in the *Gazette des Beaux Arts* for September 1878, to a hymn of hope arising with consoling tones amidst the stern realities of death.

The design (fig. 53) is masterly; the workmanship precise and accurate, without pretentious pettiness of elaboration. The subjects in

Fig. 53.—Dalmatic of Spanish embroidery.

the centre are wrought with gold threads couched in coloured silks, whilst with felicitous counterchange, the cartouches are worked with coloured silks couched in gold thread. The scrolls are of gold thread laid, and their leafy termination and fruits are of coloured silks

overstitched with gold.   The whole, from its breadth
of style, harmonious relationship of the materials in
which it is wrought, completeness of execution, and

Fig. 54.—Apparel of dalmatic in fig. 53, of Spanish embroidery.

just correlation of details, is one of the best specimens
that can be recommended for the study of this sort
of embroidery.

Another piece, probably of Spanish origin also, lovely in its details, but a little heavy in its relief, belongs to the Spitzer collection, and is a lectern cover, said to have been a gift of Charles V. to the monastery of St. Juste, in Estramadura, whither he retired to end his days in 1558. This lectern cover is a sort of long rectangular scarf of red velvet, the main portion of which is powdered over with blossom, and crossed S devices worked in gold thread. At the ends of the velvet cover are panels, the more sumptuous of which contains a figure subject. The other is blazoned in gold, with a large eagle (emblem of St. John the Evangelist), accentuated in relief and almost filling up the panel. In the spaces between its head, wings, and claws, are golden spanglings shaped like little blossoms. Upon the breast of the bird is a medallion, in which is a portrait of the saint delicately embroidered in coloured silks. The panel at the other end of the cover shows us St. John, seated in the midst of landscape scenery, writing his Gospel, inspired thereto by the Virgin who is figured in the skies above. The embroidery is well carried out, though with less refinement than one would find in a correspondingly important piece of Italian workmanship. The border around the whole cloth is composed of a pattern of repeated truncated and leafy branches.*

The date of this embroidery is that of the best period of the Flemish and Dutch schools of painting, which were noted for extraordinary care in minutely depicting detail.

In a way we may trace a similar scrupulousness

* Theodore Biais, *Gazette des Beaux Arts*, August 1874.

of execution in Flemish embroideries of this period, for which a fair justification can be pleaded from the materials so used being under more restraint than those of the painters.

Many orphreys and chasuble crosses vie with painted panels of Flemish triptychs. One selected as an illustration of this (fig. 55) is typical of the finest work of its kind. The design is a sixteenth-century version of the Jesse Tree device. King David with a long beard is in the centre ; and the character of all the figures is forcibly rendered. Supreme quality of Flemish em-

Fig. 55.—Cross or orphrey from a Flemish chasuble (in the Hochon collection).

broidery is to be seen in an altar frontal, 4.60 metres long and 1.10 wide, exhibited in the Royal Museum of Antiquities and Armour of the Porte de la Hal at Brussels. It comes from the abbey of Grimbergen, and bears the arms of Christopher Outers, prior, from 1615 to 1647.*

An inscription, *Panis confortans Christus*, indicates

Fig. 56.—The Last Supper, embroidered on a panel to an altar frontal (in the Museum of Antiquities and Armour at Brussels).

that the main idea of the design is the glorification of the mystical feast of the Eucharist. This the artist illustrates by means of a series of panels separated by

* See *Classified Documents concerning Flemish Art in the Fifteenth and Sixteenth Centuries*, Van Ysendeck.

architectural ornaments, each panel containing incidents from the Gospel, in which Jesus Christ figures as taking part in a repast of some sort.   The Last Supper

of course occupies the first place (fig. 56), then follow panels with the wedding feast in Cana of Galilee, the entertainment in Bethany in the house of Simon the leper, the repast with Zacchæus, and the dinner at Emmaus.   The architectural surroundings, and accessories couched in both glistening and burnished gold, are designed with great elegance, and modelled in gentle relief.   The grouping of the different figures in each panel is admirable ; Christ, sometimes at the centre, at others at the side of the table, is always rendered with dazzling majesty.   The faces, embroidered with utmost skill in silks, are fine and full of expression, the actions appropriate to the scene, and the attitudes nobly expressed.

Fig. 57.—Spanish relief embroidery in gold threads and coloured silks (on an orphrey from the Fortuny collection).

The specimen is in fine condition. We know of no better nor more important piece of needlework.   It is, in fact, the gem of the highly remarkable set of embroideries to be seen in the Porte de la Hal Museum.

Before this period embroidery had been done in considerable quantities with coloured threads upon canvas and on white linen articles. Linen had been somewhat rare. Queen Isabella of Bavaria had in her wedding trousseau three dozen "chemises of Holland," a quantity which seemed a great luxury to the French court.* Her spouse, Charles VI., wore silk shirts, however, one of which is recorded as of "white silk, striped with red silk and embroidered with letters of gold (1422)."

In the accounts of Margaret of France, dated 1545, we find "four livres, twelve sous (about twelve shillings), for a trimming to a chemise, ornamented with crimson silk."

White thread embroideries were hardly known; linen garments, rarely of very fine texture, were quite plain and without decoration.

But in the sixteenth century this gradually changed; the manufacture of linen was im-

Fig. 58.—Border of red silk embroidery on a linen cloth (in M. E. Bocher's collection).

proved, and finer qualities played an important part in costume, whilst other varieties were more largely used for household purposes.

Considerable numbers of towels or napkins, em-

* Bezon, *Dict. Gen. des Tissus Anc. et Mod.*, vol. viii., p. 232.

broidered with nice effect in red silk, etc., thus came into use (figs. 58, 59, and 60).

A desire for more pronounced effects of decoration in the borders of such clothes also arose. *Point coupé* (cut work) was accordingly adopted, resulting in the production of patterns with cut-out and open details, many filled in with small devices of needlework, which gave value to the more solid sections of the design about them. Through the influence of a taste for lighter and less compactly woven grounds the limits of needlework were extended, and embroidery on linen, from which certain threads had been withdrawn (*à fils tirés*), leaving such as were sufficient to carry an overcasting of stitches, came into vogue; and, later still, embroidery on net.

Fig. 59.—Border of embroidery, with devices of double-headed eagle, crown, and *fleur de lys*, to a linen cloth (in the Cluny Museum).

At this period it was the fashion for all ladies to apply themselves to embroidering. Catherine de Médicis was renowned for her skill in it. Brantôme tells us that she would gather round her her daughters, Claude, Elizabeth, and Margaret, with their cousins the Guises, and sometimes the exiled Mary Stuart, and with them "she passed a great portion of her time after dinner in silk needlework, in which she was as great an adept as possible."

Ronsard, referring to Queen Margot, sister of Francis I., writes :—

Elle adonnot son courage
A faire maint bel ouvrage
Dessus la toile, et encor
*A joindre la soye et l'or.**

But for such broideries ladies required special patterns, and drawings of these would be passed from hand to hand for each to make copies from them. Hence the circulation of patterns was somewhat slow.

Happily new inventions at this time came to the

Fig. 60.—Coloured silk embroidery on linen of the sixteenth century (in the Cluny Museum).

assistance of the ladies. Engraving on wood had been practised for a century. Maso di Finiguerra had given a new impulse to the use of engraved metal plates from which impressions could be taken, and Gutenberg issued his first proofs of printing from movable type in 1454. Such various means, of bringing writings and designs within the reach of all, were adopted early in the sixteenth century for the publication of beautiful embroidery patterns made up as pattern books. Their

* Ronsard, *Ode à la Royne de Navarre*, Book II., ode vii.

9

success was considerable; since their numbers increased as if by enchantment. In a few years
French, German, Italian, Flemish, and English publishers spread broadcast books of designs made by
their best engravers, in addition to those previously
issued.

Pierre Quinty seems to be the first of such publishers.
In 1527 appeared his " new and subtle book respecting
the art and science of making embroidery, fringes,
tapestries, as well as of other crafts done with the
needle." *

Francis Pelegrin at Paris, William Vostermans at
Angers, Claude Nourry *dit* Leprince at Lyons,
Tagliente, Nicolo d'Aristotile, Vavassore le Guadagnino
and twenty others at Venice, published in rapid suc-
cession books of ingenious and interesting patterns.

The new style of open work led to further developments of needlework, and little by little from embroidery
was evolved needlepoint lace, of which more hereafter, when we shall also go more fully into the
question of the pattern books here merely referred to
incidentally.

Many of them, and especially the earlier ones, like
that of Pierre Quinty, relate solely to embroidery;
but the arts of embroidery and lace-making, as displayed by the patterns in some of the books, frequently
merged into one another in such a way as to render the
distinctions between the several points of union difficult
of definition. Later on we shall endeavour to dis-
engage these difficulties one from the other.

* " Livre nouveau et subtil touchant l'art et science tant de brouderie
fronssures, tapisseries, còme autre mestiers quò fait à l'esguille."

Under Henry II. costume was scarcely more than a mass of embroidery. Black velvet, principally employed, was enlivened by dainty gold threads, which deviously coursed in traceries along borders, and as insertions over men's doublets and cloaks. In women's dresses the bodies, sleeves, and borders of the skirts were embroidered, and a panel, or band of similar work, ran up the front of the dress.* The more frequent ornamental devices, repeated in series, were those of reversed and interlaced S's, truncated leafy branches, and little compartments enclosing flowerets and pomegranates, dolphins and intertwisted scrolls, all of which occur in the pattern books in delightful variety. Amongst such we meet with the combined cypher of Diane de Poitiers and Henry II.

At this time, too, hand-knitting of stockings was a favourite occupation. The first pair is said to have been worn by Henry II. when he attended the marriage of his sister, Margaret of France, with Emmanuel Philibert, Duke of Savoy. Embroidery was worked on stockings as on everything else, from velvet caps to linen underclothes. When dead, the king was laid out in state, " dressed in a Holland shirt most excellently broidered about the collar and the cuffs."†

After the demise of her royal spouse, Catherine de Médicis adopted, in her mourning garb, a fanciful luxuriousness, of which we can scarcely form a conception ; amongst other things she had a mourning bed, concerning which M. Bonnaffé has gathered

---

* Carrying one back to a similar band of embroidery in the peplos of Athéné Polias (fig. 19, p. 36).

† See description by Godefroy in *Le Ceremonial de France.*

numerous particulars in following his close investigations of the queen's accounts, recorded after her
decease in 1589.   This bed was astounding in its
wealth of embroidery, as may be inferred from the
following extract :—

"A bed of black velvet, embroidered with pearls,
powdered with crescents and suns, a foot-board, head-

Fig. 61.—French embroidery in small tent and cross stitches on
canvas (in Mademoiselle de Bressolles' collection).

board, nine valances, and coverlet of state similarly
bedecked with crescents and suns; three damask curtains, with leafy wreaths and garlands figured upon a
gold-and-silver ground, and fringed along the edges
with broideries of pearls."

It stood in a chamber all hung "with rows of the
queen's devices in cut black velvet on cloth of silver."

The adjoining room was draped "with black satin, ornamented with white gimp work."

The reign of Charles IX. was melancholy with its religious warfares, and his subjects suffered great miseries. Complaints of the extravagance of the court were endless, and petitions were numerous. One, presented to Catherine de Médicis in 1586, is typical. It is entitled "An Address upon the Extreme Dearness of Living, . . . etc., presented to the mother of the king by one of her faithful servitors, Du Haillan de Bordeaux." Referring to the court circle it sets forth that "their mills, their lands, their pastures, their woods, and all their revenues are wasted upon embroideries, insertions, trimmings, tassels, fringes, hangings, gimps, needleworks, small chain stitchery, germanders, quiltings, back stitchings, etc., . . . new diversities of which are invented from day to day."

When Henry III. succeeded Charles IX. his dependents gave themselves up to an exaggeration of fashion in wearing velvets damasked with gold thread. Their ornamentation was almost always in the best taste, and this partially accounts for the employment during a protracted period of such fabrics. The same decorative motives were to be seen in men's doublets as in the delicate chasing of their daggers; sword-guards and ivory mounts to muskets repeated the favourite wreaths and garlands and scrolls, amongst which birds, dogs, and other animals disported themselves with delightful ornamental effect.

Henry III. founded the Order of the St. Esprit (31st December, 1578), the regulations of which applied to the veriest details of its ceremonials. All the knights wore costumes and mantles of red velvet embroidered with gold; the hat, mantle, doublet, and even the backs of the gloves were all worked in gold with the duly prescribed emblems of the order, the chief of which was typical of the Holy Ghost. The vestments of the clergy engaged in the religious functions of the order were also sumptuously embroidered with this emblem.

At length, however, the rage for costumes made with heavy velvets, which had been so generally worn for more than a century, came to an end; and a reaction set in in favour of brocades and brocatelles, stuffs of flowery patterns, the designs for which gave birth to the use of pomegranates and other fruits with fine foliage. The designers sought inspiration from plants blossoming in luxuriant fulness. An intelligent horti-culturalist (Jean Robin) set himself to meet the demand in this respect, by opening a garden with conservatories in which he cultivated strange varieties of plants, then but little known in our latitudes. This proved an immense success.

In a short time the king (Henry IV.) purchased Jean Robin's horticultural establishment, which, under the name of *Jardin du Roi*, became crown property. The learned Guy de la Brosse in 1626 propounded the suggestion that medical students might study the plants without interference with the designers for embroideries and tapestries; whence the first *Jardin des Plantes* (Botanical Garden), with its Natural History Museum, came into being. This institution seemed so excellent that every country adopted it as an example and founded similar ones. Who would have thought it possible for embroidery thus to have come to the aid of science!

But, as may be easily divined, taste for showy stuffs could but stimulate the wild expenses incurred by great nobles. In spite of the personal simplicity observed by good King Henry IV., and the austere disposition of his minister Sully, fops and exquisites took advantage of public ceremonies to uphold luxurious displays, at times carried to amazing excess. Bassompierre, in his *Memoires*, tells how, for the baptism of Louis XIII., he had a costume made of flowered cloth of gold bedizened with so many pearls that they alone cost 8,000 écus, not to mention 6,000 écus for the stuffs and the making of the clothes, in all 14,000 écus, or about 167,000 francs (£6,680) of current coin.

Henry IV., opposed to this courtly folly, issued several edicts against " the glitterings and gildings."

But the most important of such edicts was that by Louis XIII., in 1629, bearing the title " Regulation of Superfluity in Clothes." This law put a limit to expenditure for costume and for the table. Article 133 is interesting here on account of its enumeration of the ornamental articles then worn. It runs :—

" We forbid men and women to wear in any way whatsoever embroidery on cloth or flax, imitations of embroidery, of bordering made up with cloth and thread, and of cutwork for ' rebatos,' capes, sleeves, done upon quintain and other linens, laces, ' passamaynes,' and other threadwork made with bobbins.

" And we forbid the use of all other ornaments upon capes, sleeves, and other linen garments, save trimmings, cutwork, and laces manufactured in this country which do not exceed at most the price of three pounds the ell, that is, for the band and its trimmings together, without evasion ;

" Upon pain of confiscation of the aforesaid capes, chainworks, collars, hats, and mantles which may be found upon offending persons ; as well as the coaches and horses which may be found similarly bedecked."

It is almost impossible to believe that such a sumptuary law was either seriously enforced or respected, in the face of the pleasing and numerous engravings of costume published at this date by Abraham Bosse, which we shall have to discuss more amply in the section on laces.

Fig. 62.—Embroidered ammunition pouch of the time of Louis XIII. (in the Cluny Museum).

Moreover, these edicts really concerned embroideries at court only, and did not affect those on ecclesiastical vestments, the output of which was always considerable. Louis XIII., on the advice of his famous minister, Cardinal Richelieu, must have been careful to avoid doing anything to militate against the production of such rich ecclesiastical adornments. We even find in the *Théâtre d'Honneur*, published in 1620 by André Favyn, a description of superb religious vestments, etc., made to the order of the king in 1619, by his Majesty's embroiderer Alexandre Paynet, for presentation to the Church of the Holy Sepulchre at Jerusalem.

As a specimen of the character of ecclesiastical work done at this period we give a cut (fig. 63) of a handsome chasuble, belonging to Messrs. Tassinari and Chatel, on which, set in massive gold couchings, are medallions wrought in coloured silks.

Louis XIV. gave the highest encouragement to embroidery; its splendour in house decorations, on furniture and costume, surpassed that previously displayed.

The wondrous luxury at Versailles dazzled the whole of Europe; but the gorgeousness of many details in it overshot the bounds of good taste, and was monstrous in exaggeration. There were, for instance, gold embroidered caryatid figures in the king's apartment measuring fifteen feet high, and proportionately bold in relief. Such a substitution of embroidery for decoration, which should have been executed rather in metal or wood carving, was clearly a mistake. A textile fabric and threads are not materials appropriate to a design of this nature. And no matter what amount of skill may have been involved in embroidering them, we cannot acquiesce in Saint Aubin's statement that these Louis XIV. caryatids were "specimens of masterwork beyond eulogy."

The king, however, showed better taste in matters of costume, and the blue uniforms which he recognized as "regulation uniforms" (fig. 64) were pleasing in appearance. In 1664 an order was issued that the right of wearing them would be granted only by special favour

Fig. 63.—Cross or orphrey on the back of a cope of Louis XIII.'s period, embroidered in gold and silver (in the collection of Messrs. Tassinari and Chatel).

of the king, and on a licence signed by himself! The number of wearers was limited; and when one died another was appointed.

The coat was of blue, lined with red, embroidered with a fine pattern in gold picked out with silver; metal spangles were freely scattered between the forms. Given the sparkling saloons in which these uniforms were worn, the golden equipages which conveyed the

Fig. 64.—Design of the embroidery on regulation uniforms (Louis XIV.), after St. Aubin.

wearers, and the magnificence of the scene is easily pictured.

Louis XIV. had many embroiderers attached to his household; and we find in the list of his domestic officers, amongst those of his hereditary grooms of the chamber, the names of Jean le Boyteux, Jacques Remy, Jean Henry, and his son Etienne Henry, all embroiderers.

On the 2nd June, 1679, Jacques Remy receives a payment of 4,000 livres (about £200), "on account of embroidered brocade, which he was making for the king," a typical instance of the important commissions given to such workmen.

Besides the above-mentioned embroiderers specially retained for the king's service, his Majesty employed others at the Gobelins factory where their workrooms adjoined those of the tapestry-makers. These were Simon Fayette and Philibert Balland, who were engaged upon the embroidering of the hangings, door and other curtains and coverings for furniture of all sorts. Fayette's speciality was for figures, whilst Balland's was for landscapes.[*]

The designs for their work was supplied by the king's designers : Bailly, who painted in miniature, Bonnemer de Falaise, Testelin, and Boulongne the younger.

Their names frequently recur in the accounts for the king's buildings.[†] We give a few extracts from those of the years 1671 and following :—

" Paid to Testelin for a painting of Jupiter on his eagle, to be used as a pattern for embroidery, 300 livres (or £15).

" To Fayette, for works in which he embroidered the figures, 2,345 livres (about £117).

" To Balland, for works in which he embroidered the landscapes, 2,855 livres (about £143).

" To Balland, for embroideries representing the capture of birds in flight, 400 livres (or £20).

" To Boulongne, for drawings of birds, 72 livres (or £3).

* A.-L. Lacordaire, *Notice Historique sur les Gobelins.*
† Jules Guiffrey, *Comptes des Bâtiments du Roi.*

"To Bonnemer, painter, for six paintings upon vellum, used as patterns for the furniture embroideries in the gallery at Versailles, 300 livres (or £15)."

Other evidence indicates the lavish expenditure incurred by the king for woven fabrics used in his palace at Versailles. We find Berain furnishing the design for a figured velvet which the king ordered from a weaver of St. Maur at a cost of 1,000 livres (or £50) the ell! Its manufacture was so intricate and slow that only a few ells of it were completed before the king died.

But the patterns of these fine fabrics, magnificent tapestries, and sumptuous embroideries were all of a grandiose style. The noble attitudes of the persons depicted in them, the bold ornamental forms, the luxuriance of flowers, the excellent selection of emblems always clear and straightforward in their symbolism, such as royal suns, helmets, swords, standards, and triumphal trumpets, all contributed to a greatness of style, which is still impressive.

Amongst the emblems thus embroidered occurs the bâton of the Marshal of France, the shape in which it was then designed being retained to the present time. It is a staff eighteen inches long, covered with blue velvet and embroidered in gold satin stitch with thirty-six *fleurs de lys*. The name of the marshal and date of his appointment are engraved upon the gold ferrule on the end of the staff.

The admirable portraits by Hyacinthe Rigaud, Largillière, and many others, which have been faithfully engraved by Nanteuil, Léonard Gautier, and Pierre Simon, supply us with accurate pictorial information

as to minutest particulars in the beautiful embroidery
used during this brilliant period upon costumes.

Ladies' dresses were generally less flowered and
bedecked with gold work than men's. With a refined
taste, women gave preference to wearing soft and fine-
textured linens, white embroideries, and thread laces,
so becoming to the skin. Persons having a taste for
real elegance ridiculed the ostentatious gold trimmings
and embroideries. Here, for example, is some of
Madame de Sévigné's delightful banter about them :—
" M. de Langlée has given Madame de Montespan a
dress of gold upon gold, wrought over with gold, with
hems of gold, and then over it a curling additional
embroidery of one gold mixed with another certain
gold, making altogether the most divine fabric that
I could possibly have imagined !!! Fairies certainly
made all this in secret."

But it should not be supposed that in the midst of
this abundant luxury women were indolent and displayed no taste in the choice and making of embroideries. Of Madame de Maintenon it is said that
she herself worked at embroidery, not only in her
apartments, but when out walking or driving. "Hardly
fairly ensconced in her carriage," according to a letter
of the time, "and before the coachman had flicked his
horses, this good lady put on her spectacles and
pulled her needlework out of the bag she carried with
her."

Then again, when the college at St. Cyr was under
her direction, Madame de Maintenon devoted the
greater measure of her efforts towards having the
young and aristocratic girls in the school instructed

in embroidery, and a quaint print now in the *Biblio-thèque Nationale* displays her, surrounded by pupils, holding pieces of needlework, and grouped, by stand-ards of difficulty suited to schoolgirls, of one, two, or three years' training. There can be little doubt that work by three years' pupils is still to be seen in the palace at Fontainebleau, on the hangings in Madame de Maintenon's apartment. These hangings, em-broidered at St. Cyr, are covered with Chinese scenes upon a jonquil yellow ground.

Fig. 65.—Indian coloured embroidery (in the Cluny Museum).

Workboxes and delicious little cases for scissors, needles, and thimbles, de-positories special to a lady's boudoir known as *bonheur du jour*, etc., reveal the fact, as testified by specimens of them in collections, that many ladies did not disdain employing some part of their leisure in the art of the needle.

Europe followed the lead of France in the fashion of embroideries, and never perhaps had so enormous a quantity of costly specimens been consumed.

On its part, the East continued to put forth needle-work of fantastic splendour. When Sobieski, King of

Poland, overcame the Turks in 1683, compelling them to raise the siege of Vienna, he took possession of a canopy hung with curtains, beneath which the Koran and Mahomet's standard had been reverentially kept in the Turkish camp. It was made of Smyrna gold brocade, embroidered in turquoises and pearls, with verses from the Koran. Its supports were of silver-gilt, beautifully chased and profusely set with enamelled and jewelled medallions. Sobieski had it converted into a state bed, which at his death was valued at 700,000 Tournese livres.

An interesting attempt was made at this period to induce the Chinese to imitate in embroidery the great decorative tapestry hangings that Louis XIV. had hung on the walls of his palaces. It seems probable that embroidery was producible in the far East at a minimum cost, and so tempted the enterprise of Portuguese or Dutch merchants, who were almost the only traders with these distant parts. Vasco de Gama was the first to double the Cape of Good Hope, and disembarked at Calcutta in May 1498. A hundred years later, in 1602, the Dutch had united under one powerful *Compagnie des Grandes Indes* all the associations which had been formed to deal in the products of the then little-known Asiatic countries.

Colbert, aiming at a greater extension of French export trade, gave every encouragement to shipowners at Marseilles, Bordeaux, Rochefort, St. Malo, and Havre, to found a *Compagnie des Indes*, which should compete with the Portuguese and Dutch. And it may have been under his directions that commissions were given to the Chinese to make embroideries on large cloths previously prepared with drawings and paintings of figure subjects, such as those done by eminent painters like Le Brun and his pupils.

There are some important door hangings at the Cluny Museum, in the borders of which are French *fleurs de lys* intermixed with Indian ornament (fig. 66). Other parts of them more whimsical in effect were probably left

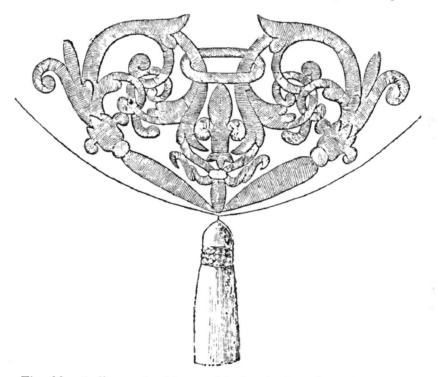

Fig. 66.--Indian embroidery, with the device of the *fleur de lys* introduced (in the Cluny Museum).

blank by the designers, and the embroiderers accordingly worked over them as their own taste dictated ; whence it happens that persons with distinctly European poses and actions are represented as wearing clothes, and moving in scenery and amongst surroundings all decorated or treated in a Chinese style. Incomplete as these experiments really are, we felt that it would be

wrong to ignore them, since the effort made by those
undertaking them was very considerable.

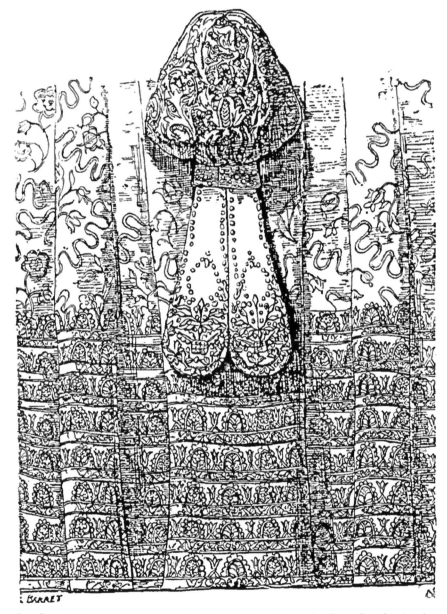

Fig. 67.—Velvet costume embroidered in gold and silver for Catherine
of Brandebourg, seventeenth century (in the Buda-Pesth Museum).

Looking back we see that the sixteenth and seventeenth centuries are periods of great splendour in

embroidery. No temerity was wanting on the part of those giving orders for all sorts of needlework ; and workers of marvellous aptitude and dexterity in France, Italy, Spain, and Flanders were always to be found, capable of carrying out the unconditional and almost priceless commissions given to them. The patrons of embroidery at this time may be occasionally charged with the reproach of having instigated the production of articles exaggerated in character, and of having indulged an inordinate craving for effect of unstinted and tawdry pretentiousness, which beguiled workers into an unhealthy style. Still, embroidery of this period, on the whole, attained a condition of perfection which leaves the bulk of that subsequently produced far in the lurch.

CHAPTER VI.

FROM LOUIS XV. TO THE PRESENT TIME.

THE character of ornament and decoration during the reign of Louis XV., which commenced under the inauspicious influence of the Regency, reflected the dissolute tone in manners developed at that period. It consequently stands in marked contrast with the breadth of style that had obtained in the previous reign. Dignity of warlike pageants and pomp of regal majesty now virtually disappeared; and pencil and needle were called upon to set forth with frothy effeminacy the triumphs of love. All artistic work dwindled and shrank in aim, and embroideries of course did not escape from the prevalent demoralization. But ladies' toilettes more especially became vehicles for a thousand and one little fripperies, most of which verged upon the grotesque. Queen Marie-Leczinska— a very thin dame—set a fashion of wearing hoops of great circumference beneath her petticoats. And one of the more extraordinary instances of such enormities is referred to by the Marquise de Créquy, in the description she gives of her grandmother's costume,—the Duchesse de la Ferté, a celebrated and extravagant woman of fashion. The Marquise writes that her grandmother wore a dress of reddish brown velvet, the skirt of which, adjusted in graceful folds, was held up by big butterflies made of Dresden china. The front was a tablier of cloth of silver, upon which was embroidered an orchestra of musicians, arranged in a pyramidal group, consisting of a series of six ranks of performers, with musical instruments wrought in raised needlework. The skirt was supported upon a hoop four ells and a half in circumference.* The Marquise averred that the cheeks of the musicians were as big as plums, from which the scale of the other parts can be fairly imagined.

Men's clothes, on the other hand, were of a more rational type. The broidered coats, and especially the daintily ornamented waistcoats, on which elegant little flowery sprays gracefully trickled about buttonholes, along pockets, and over trimmings of cuffs, are notice-able amongst the more pleasant results of the art of embroidery at this time. As taste in such matters became refined, it was difficult to satisfy the exactions which consequently arose for very delicate execution in tiny details. This tendency led many nobles, pedantic amateurs of this class of embroidery, to remain satisfied no longer with what European workmen could do for them. Accordingly many sent their clothes, ready cut out, to be embroidered in China (fig. 68). St. Aubin writes that at his time embroideries done with fine and evenly whipped cords or gimps came into fashion. "This," he says, "we owe to the Chinese, by whom many embroideries, most precise in regularity, have been made for fanciful dandies." The importation of this excellent Chinese work was the means of securing for us many

* *Souvenirs de la Marquise de Créquy*, vol. i., p. 205.

of those fascinating coats of the period of Louis XV. and Louis XVI., which no one tires of admiring (figs. 68, 69, 70, and 72).

Never, perhaps, will *finesse* in embroidery be carried further. Floss and spun silks were made up into different kinds of threads, such as gimps, and chenilles, and even small narrow ribands like those used on book tassels, and these varieties were intermixed in embroideries. Gold and silver was employed not only in smooth threads, but also for granulated ones, and as beads and spangles of all sizes, as wires, and little bars, in laminations, in bullion, as frizzed threads for chain-stitch work, and narrow flat braids. The number of stitches increased in a remarkable way.

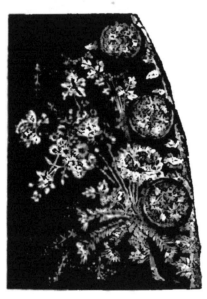

Fig. 68.—Embroidery in Chinese style upon a coat of the eighteenth century (in the Museum of Decorative Arts).

On the other hand we meet with specimens of work most curious in their close resemblance to embroidery, and yet entirely made without a single needle stitch. The method of producing them seems to have been as follows :— Over an engraving, fixed to a card, a layer of transparent adhesive wax mixture was floated on with a brush. The card thus prepared was then placed upon the hot plate of a chafing-dish, so as to render the wax soft and bring the other adhesive ingredients into a gently melting state. Flat silk threads could then be applied to the lines of the engraving as seen through the transparent glue. By pressing them with a nail of the finger or a small instrument the flat silk threads were made to adhere to the surface, being carried backwards and forwards from right to left and left to right and laid close to one another, over the portion to be covered with the same coloured silk. When carefully done, the illusion is complete, and conveys the

Fig. 69.—Embroidered pocket of a satin waistcoat of the eighteenth century (in the Museum of Decorative Arts).

impression of flat embroidery in fine silk. Skin textures were obviously very difficult of treatment in this manner, consequently, wherever they occurred in the engraving, blank spaces were as a rule left, which were subsequently painted in water-colour. This process, as will have been seen, is fantastic and ingenious, but scarcely commendable as an artistic substitute for embroidery.

A great deal of wool work on canvas (cross and tent stitch) was done in the eighteenth century. It is easy of execution, the stitches are counted and taken according to the meshes, but the results of the work are rarely artistic.

Fig. 70.—Embroidery in gold and pearls upon the wedding coat of the "Grand Dauphin," after St. Aubin.

Seats, which before Louis XIII.'s time had generally but little stuffing in them or trimming on them, were considerably upholstered under Louis XIV. But appetite for anything contributing to luxurious ease and comfort was prodigiously developed under Louis XV., and a great quantity of seats in shapes hitherto unknown were then produced : sofas, *causeuses* (small sofas), *tête-à-têtes*, or double seats, came into use, and were covered with tapestry-weavings or with canvas embroidered in cross and tent-counted stitches.

When human figures were part of the ornamentation in this class of work they were done with silks in very small cross and tent stitches. Furniture embroideries so made in the time of Louis XIV. are notable for rich flowery patterns and ornamental details of a bold style (fig. 71). Under Louis XV. grotesque forms, monkeys, squirrels, clowns, and such-like at times pourtrayed with great spirit, very finely worked, but often in very mediocre taste, were freely adopted. François Boucher, when appointed court

Fig. 71.—Chair covered with superb embroidery, of the end of the
seventeenth century.

painter, supplied pastoral designs which, however mannered, were always elegant.

This counted stitch work on canvas is the easiest of all embroideries, and many fashionable women applied themselves to it. Marie Antoinette herself, with Madame Elisabeth, commenced some work of this sort, which she intended for her apartments on the ground-floor of the Louvre, but its completion was cut short

Fig. 72.—Embroidery with spangles and tinsel for a coat, Louis XVI. period (in the Museum of Art and Industry at Lyons).

by the Revolution. The specimens themselves were, at the commencement of the Empire period, exhibited on sale at Mademoiselle Dubucquois', who had been purveyor to the queen.*

Returning to the period of Louis XV. we must make special mention of a circumstance giving rise to an unwonted output of embroidery. A chapter of the

---

* Comte de Reiset, *Livre Journal de Madame Etoffe*, vol. i., p. 478.

Order of the St. Esprit had not been held since the reign of Henry III., so the king decided to celebrate with much ceremony a general reassemblage of the knights and officers of the order. His embroiderer (Rocher) was commissioned to produce a magnificent throne. Three hundred workwomen were employed for many months in embroidering the stuffs for its canopy, hangings, and coverings. Emblems of the St. Esprit, interchanged with *fleurs de lys*, were scattered over the grounds, whilst the borders were rich in gold work. The vestments of the officiating clergy were thickly embroidered with gold, and powdered over with St. Esprits in silver. In the *Memoires Secrets* of Bachaumont the value of these embroideries is placed at more than three hundred thousand livres.

Princely nuptials were also occasions for the giving of important orders for embroideries (fig. 70). La Fage, Jean Perreux, and Trumeau are cited as having been engaged by the Duc de Choiseul to embroider satin fittings and linings of superb coaches used in the wedding *cortège* of the Grand Dauphin when he married Marie-Joseph of Saxony.

Monsieur de Montgomery contributed to the exhibition of the *Union Centrale des Arts Decoratifs* held in 1882 a bed and arm-chair worked in feather stitch, which had belonged to Queen Marie-Leczinska. The canopy and head of the bed are decorated with medallions, containing subjects such as Psyche rising and looking at Cupid. Upon the coverlet are Cupid, Jupiter, and Mercury.

A very marked impulse was given to the Lyons silk manufactories in the eighteenth century, and to embroideries made in that town. The designers for them displayed high skill in their compositions; particularly two, Bony an inhabitant, previously at Gisors, and Philippe de la Salle, both of whom left behind them a great reputation.[*]

Linen was of a most exquisite quality, consonant with this age of frivolity. Inimitable skill was shown in embroidering delicate cambrics, with which coquettish duchesses, equally punctilious in their dishabille as in their *grandes toilettes*, would envelop themselves. The needle-workers of Saxony were conspicuous for the excellence of their drawn thread and all sorts of white embroideries; and the Queen and the Dauphin set a fashion for these as well as for porcelain wares from Saxony.

The rococo style, which had its vogue in the reign of Louis XV., was based upon the employment of forms like conch and other shells nestling amongst frizzy mosses and imaginary rocks, joined together by ornaments of fantastic shape, but of absolutely false construction. Under Louis XVI. a tentative reaction towards classic ornament was manifested. Greek friezes and wreathings, daintily drawn by Salembier and other able designers of the eighteenth century, encouraged the adoption of a purer style in treating floral decoration. Tulips, carnations, and roses, tied with coloured ribands of tender tones, surrounded medallions edged with bead ornaments, from which depended garlands mixed with groups, or trophies of sylvan and mythological attributes. Such devices embroidered on satin produced refined and elegant

* Bezon, *Dictionnaire des Tissus*, vol. iv., p. 253.

effects, especially when used in conjunction with baskets garnished with ribands, *motifs*, which find frequent imitations at the present day.

The Revolution closed this volatile century, and gave melancholy employment to embroiderers in setting them to pull to pieces the finest and most beautiful work of antecedent times. It is not without a sense of sorrow that one reads of forty or fifty needlewomen, at Angers, in Vendemaire, of the year 3, being engaged to carefully unpick and spoil the various pieces of a set of embroideries, such as the valances of a bed or of a canopy, in order, as it was asserted, to make the restoration of them by persons attached to the old *régime* all the more difficult. These work-women were compelled to unstitch braids and all articles in which gold and silver thread had been used, which were then sent to the smelting pots for the benefit of the nation. Circumstances of this de-scription caused the destruction of the fine specimens known since the time of René d'Anjou as the great embroidery of Messire Saint-Maurice. The art of the needle thereby suffered an irreparable loss, the reality of which gains in vividness if one recalls the facts that certain velvet copes, bereft of their golden figures, orphreys, and laces, were even then purchased at prices from 695 to 800 livres (about £27 to £32), the bids for those disposed of at a single sale alone amounting to 24,350 livres (or £1,217).

When the tumult and horrors of the Revolution, so inimical to the gentle pursuits of embroideresses, had subsided, bees, in lieu of *fleurs de lys*, were abundantly embroidered ; but as wars virtually absorbed the attention and energies of the nation during the Empire, embroidery received scanty recognition and encouragement. Comparatively few of such handsome costumes and uniforms as are painted by Gérard in his portraits of Napoleon, Joséphine, and Marie-Louise were to be seen in the saloons of the imperial court (fig. 73).

At the coronation of Charles X. the robes of state were profusely worked with gold, as the big picture of the ceremony, now at Versailles, shows us ; but on

Fig. 73.—Silver spangle embroidery for a coat, Empire period
(in the Museum of Decorative Arts).

passing into a few rooms further on, similar pictures of the splendid functions, under Louis XIV., will be found significantly emphasizing the decadence which, meanwhile, had ensued and culminated in later phases of poor artistic needlework.

Within the last fifty years works of embroidery have been very widely diffused, and their use adopted amongst all classes of society, as well as in countries which follow European fashions. Development of commercial relations has singularly favoured the life of the industry, though much more so as regards quantity than beauty of production.

It may be safely stated that embroidered ornaments have been, and are still, very considerably applied to costume, house decoration, and furniture.

The East has of late years sent us, by numerous and easy modes of transit, marvels of old-time and traditional art, with which Europe has been but little acquainted.

Not only have we been supplied with lovely Persian and Turkish carpets, but from the valley of Cashmere we have received stores of shawls, some wonderfully woven, others embroidered with the characteristic and exquisitely soft wool (or pushmena) that eclipses any analogous material. India has sent us muslins finely worked with gold thread palmates and stitched over with iridescent beetle's wings. Théophile Gautier, in a passage full of colour, thus conveys the impression he received from Oriental embroideries :—

" It might almost be said that Indian embroidery seeks to engage in a contest with the sun, to have a duel to the death with the blinding light and glowing sky; it attempts to shine as brilliantly beneath this fiery deluge; it realizes the wonders of fairy tales ; it produces dresses in colours of the weather, of the sun, of the moon ; metals, flowers, precious stones, lustres, beams of light, and flashes are mixed upon its incandescent palette. Over a silvery net it makes wings of beetles to vibrate like fluttering golden emeralds. With the scales of beetles' bodies it gives birth to impossible foliage mixed with flowers of diamonds. It avails itself of the shimmer of tawny silk, of the opalescent hues of

mother-of-pearl, of the splendid gold blue blendings of
the peacock's plumage. It disdains nothing, not even
tinsel, provided it flashes brightly ; not even crystal, so
long as it irradiates light. At all costs its duty is to

Fig. 74.—Slavonic peasant's cap embroidered in gold, eighteenth
century (in Monsieur G. Bapst's collection).

shine, sparkle, and glitter, to send forth prismatic rays ;
it must be blazing, blinding, and phosphorescent; and
so the sun acknowledges its defeat."*

* Théophile Gautier's *l'Orient à l'Exposition*, quoted by Didron in
his *Report upon the Decorative Arts*, 1878.

What more could this glowing writer have said had he even seen the astounding splendours of the specimen presented some forty years ago to Mahomet's tomb by Kinderao, Rajah of Baroda? It was a *chadar* or veil composed entirely of inwrought pearls and precious stones, disposed in an arabesque pattern, and said to have cost a crore of rupees (a million pounds). Although the richest stones were worked into it the effect was most harmonious. When spread out in the sun it seemed suffused with a general iridescent pearly bloom, as grateful to the eyes as were the exquisite forms of its arabesques.*

China and Japan have flooded the markets of Europe with their silks, vivaciously embroidered with sympathetically designed natural objects. By the side of Chinese robes, ornamented with the imperial dragon, so *chatoyant* in tint, with its green-toned golds, one equally admires Japanese *foukouses*, "those squares of stuff, more or less worked over, which are used by the Japanese as covers to their ceremonial gifts; the plumage of birds is above all rendered upon them with exquisite feeling, the tones and surface effects of silk being subtly employed in securing surprising effects of colours" (fig. 75).

Georgians and Greeks work charming meanders upon cloth in gold threads or cords, picked out sometimes with small discs or little coins.

To the East again we must turn for the best embroideries produced during the first half of our century. Excepting some few good imitations of ancient work, there is little to engage our attention in the masses of

* *The Industrial Arts of India*, by Sir George Birdwood, vol. ii., p. 118.

European embroidery produced at that time.   France,
Switzerland, Saxony, and the United Kingdom have

Fig. 75.—Embroidered Japanese foukouse or cover (in the
Montefiore collection).

employed native talent in the art, but with alternations
of success and discouragement.*   All sorts of needlework

* Felix Aubry *Report on the London Exhibition of* 1851.

have been successively attempted, especially such as are
easy of execution. Fashion has capriciously inclined to
one or other of them, evoking, during the periods of its
heat, enormous quantities of hurried work, often designed
with spirit, but almost always deficient in that quality
of persevering care and conviction, the impress of which
is always seen in a work of real art. Quick work and
cheap labour especially, heedlessness of the particular
use to which an embroidery is to be put, attempt to
make it do equally well for a church, for a bit of furniture, or a dress, are elements which invariably militate
against style in workmanship.

The machine invented by the Alsatian Hellmann has
in latter years supplied what is wanted for the superficial requirements of present days. By ingenious
mechanism a hundred double-pointed needles, threaded
in the middle, are made to pass backwards and forwards
through a vertically stretched textile. Little carriages
fitted with nippers seize the needles as they emerge
through the stuff, thus playing the part of hands to pull
through and return the needles, almost in the same
way as the manipulation described in chap. i., p. 6.
The bars on which the stuff is fixed in the machine are
brought into relation with a pantograph and are adjusted
accordingly for each stitch, so that the stuff can be
shifted in any direction, as the requirements of the
design render necessary. This machine is very cleverly
devised, and produces results that satisfy a demand for
effective and low-priced goods.

But, confronted with such a formidable rival, is the art
of embroidery to be lost to such supple and submissive
fingers as those which in bygone times realized with

devotion and toil the lovely needleworks we have endeavoured to describe in the foregoing pages ? Are mechanical processes ceaselessly pouring forth abundant quantities of things to supplant artistic handicrafts ? Well-cared-for handworks have, however, always been, and presumably always will be, wanted where mere hasty selection of patterns is not the only exercise of artistic taste. Concurrently with the extraordinary development of mechanical processes, there is a wide-spread movement in favour of closer study of artistic works of past periods. Artists furnish their studios with ancient stuffs, and tapestries and embroideries of great age are rescued from beneath the accumulations of dust where, since the last century, public apathy left them. Thus the exercise of the art of embroidery, and an appreciation of its possibilities, are stimulated, and new and delightful phases of the art manifest themselves.

Many persons have acquired portions of those picturesque costumes formerly beloved in their respective provinces, but now fast disappearing before the relentless current of modern customs. Breton waistcoats, Norman caps, Alsatian coifs glistening with gold, have been sought for and obtained in France and abroad by intelligent collectors, who prize them for their excellence as objects of study and as remains of local art stamped with originality and character (figs. 47 and 80).

Under a cultivated guidance skilful embroiderers have zealously reproduced well-chosen, genuine, and typical specimens of old-time embroidery (fig. 76). Encouraged by success in this direction, and emulating methods in vogue during the best epochs of embroidery, all who have seriously engaged their talents in producing ornamental broideries for furniture or costume, have at length ventured into the confines of the higher branches of the art.

Chasuble-makers now produce ecclesiastical ornaments worthy to be used in our cathedrals side by side with the scarce relics preserved from the despoiling

Fig. 76.—Reproduction of a sixteenth century embroidery in gold and coloured silks, by M. Henry.

touch of revolutions. The mitre, figured with the Crucifixion (fig. 78), wrought in feather stitch with coloured silks upon a tissue of gold and enriched with, pearls, and the peacock-blue rep cover, set with crystal bosses, for the Papal Bull of the Immaculate Conception (fig. 79), are works which reflect honour upon our time.

Tapestry-weavers and upholsterers make coverings

and embroideries for furniture incomparably superior in design and suitability to those twenty years ago.*

But more marked improvements are seen in fancy work.   Instead of the conventional square of canvas covered with a cross-stitch parrot or a horrible

Fig. 77.—Small screen of modern embroidery, by M. Henry.

little dog, work of charming design and good workmanship is produced.   Every assiduous woman now embroiders in satin stitch, feather stitch, check or chessboard stitch, and *point de Hongrie* (Hungary stitch); whilst those having greater skill do *petit point* (small

---

* We would call attention to the very remarkable modern embroideries with the verses of the *Credo*, made for the stalls of the Cologne Cathedral.

cross and tent stitch), various sorts of couching, and
shading stiches; they lay and stitch down traceries
of gold thread about panels and medallions, as was

Fig. 78.—Mitre figured with the Crucifixion, embroidered by Biais.

done in the sixteenth century, or represent playfully
twining ribands as in the eighteenth century.

Thus it comes to pass that, in the presence of records of

knowledge and of specimens brought together by modern
eclecticism, in a way that no other age has attempted,
and composed of ingatherings from the East and the
West, from primitive and polished civilizations, arranged

Fig. 79.—Embroidered cover made tor the Papal Bull of the
Immaculate Conception, by Biais.

in museums, and representative of all ages and peoples,
the embroiderer of the present day finds himself plen-
teously provided with exceptional means for taking a
great step forward in the progress of his art.

Called upon to take part in such an advance, we have written these pages, convinced that they coincide with the dawn of a great epoch in the art of the needle. A fixed intention of reviving the noble, but too long forgotten traditions of embroidery, manifests itself every day in France, England, Germany, Hungary, Italy—in

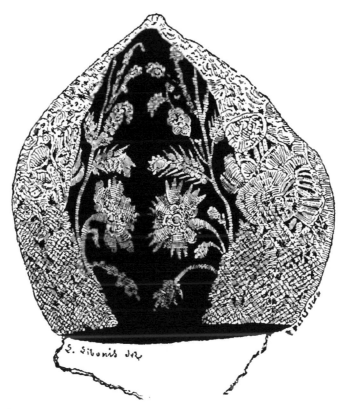

Fig. 80.—Alsatian peasant's cap embroidered in gold on black velvet (in Monsieur G. Bapst's collection).

fact, everywhere. A justification of our hopes is therefore clearly found in the general movement alluded to.

We feel certain that many women, especially the better educated, will become more and more conversant with the artistic delights derivable from the use of their needles. That they will grow to love the "needle's excellency," and find this incomparable little instrument always willing to translate with variety of stitches, designs, or paintings which shall ornament a textile and give it desirable attributes. But there must be no scamped or superficial work; the machine can always beat that. On the contrary, let us strive to perfect methods of the handicraft; and in such a manner that the artist, having made his sketch on paper, shall not disdain to transfer his design to the stuff on which it is to be wrought, to consider the colours to be used in it, the reliefs, details, spangles, beads, gold threads, or whatever appears to him to be necessary for it; nor to delegate the transfer of his design to some prentice hand which shall, as has too often been the case, contort the shapes and curves of his composition. As a matter of the highest importance, utmost care in drawing patterns and selecting materials should be thoroughly inculcated at all schools of artistic needlework. Under such guarded circumstances the success of the embroideress is better assured.

We have endeavoured to bring before our readers salient features of the history of Embroidery. And our aim is attained, firstly, if we have successfully demonstrated that no superior process for the decoration of textiles exists; and, secondly, if we have been able to do justice to those humble workwomen too frequently neglected and left to starve by a public, which haggles over the acquisition of the earlier marvels of the needleworker's art, and yet, when modern work is in question, gives preference to the showy but altogether less artistic embroideries produced by machinery.

PART II.—LACES.

NEEDLEPOINT LACE.

CHAPTER I.

THE SIXTEENTH CENTURY — TRANSITION FROM EMBROIDERY TO NEEDLEPOINT LACE-MAKING.

THERE are two classes of laces: those made with a needle, and those made with bobbins on a pillow. We shall consider needlepoint laces first, since their analogy with embroideries, whence they are derived, entitles them to the precedence given them in this book.

Lace, whether of needlepoint or pillow make, is a textile fabric with open-work grounds ; and both the ornament and the ground are entirely produced by the lace-maker. Needlepoint lace is made by first stitching thread along the outlines of a pattern drawn on paper or parchment, by which means a skeleton thread pattern is produced. This skeleton threadwork serves as the scaffolding, as one might call it, upon and between which the stitches, for the shapes and ground between them, are cast and so wrought into needlepoint lace.

With these few words of definition, let us now enter upon the history of this industry.

Origin.—All authors on the subject have attempted

to show when the making of lace was commenced. Some, dealing in a summary way with this question, have stated that the origin of the work is lost in the mists of early time; but that, according to certain expressions found in Greek and Latin writings, lace-making may be supposed to have been practised in the classic periods of industry.

But successive and more precise researches made by the principal of modern writers—Felix Aubry, Mrs. F. Bury-Palliser, Alan S. Cole, and J. Seguin—leave little room for doubting that there is no documentary or reliable evidence to prove the existence of lace before the fifteenth century.

In the East, the cradle of our industries, light tissues, such as gauzes, and muslins, and nets (see fig. 81), were undoubtedly made at very early times, and were used as veils and scarfs, etc., after the manner of subsequent laces; and women enriched them with some sort of embroidery (fig. 82), or varied the openness of them by here and there drawing out threads.

With a view to variety and ornament early makers of fringes plaited and knotted the threads of them; and it is also probable that they may have tied them together or worked stitches upon them, since such work might plausibly answer to the description of ancient trimmings for the *scutulata vestis*, a sort of Roman toga, of which the borders, according to Dupont-Auberville, were of open reticulated weaving.*

But, whatever may be said, we do not, in these, recognize lace, the production of which involves much

* See *L'Ornement des Tissus*, by Dupont-Auberville and Victor Gay.

more refined and artistic methods, and postulates a combination of skill and varied
execution carried to a higher
degree of perfection.

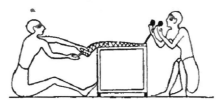

Fig. 81.--Egyptians making net (from Wilkinson's *Ancient Egyptians*).

The monk Reginald, who
took part in opening the
tomb of St. Cuthbert at
the cathedral of Durham in
the twelfth century, writes that the Saint's shroud had

Fig. 82.—A net-work embellished with glass beads (Egyptian Museum of the Louvre).

a fringe of linen threads an inch long;
surmounted by a border " worked upon
the threads " with representations of birds
and pairs of beasts, there being between
each such pair a branching tree. This
tree was a survival of the sacred Oriental
" hom " tree, previously mentioned. But
from this description of the work no one
can decisively say that it was a species
of open stitched embroidery;* and not
before the end of the fifteenth century do
we find indications of such open embroidery becoming the staple production
of a specialized industry.

We explained in the history of embroidery how luxury in the use of fine
textiles was developed after the Crusades,
when princes and kings stimulated the
manufacture of silken stuffs. Velvets and silks came

* The contemporary MS. by Reginald the Monk speaks of this
border to the winding-sheet as being " inwoven," and seems to suggest
that the weaving produced equally good effects on the back and front
of the material; not, therefore, that the fabric was consequently in
the nature of an open-work or ornamental net.

to be the habitual materials for the costumes of lords

Fig. 83.—Cutwork (*point coupe*) sixteenth century
(*Musée des Arts décoratifs*).

and their ladies.　Linens in Brittany, those too of

Alençon and Lille, and more especially of Holland, were made in finer qualities ; and luxury in using them succeeded to. that of employing other costly and heavier fabrics.

Embroideries with open grounds. — Embroidered linen consequently came into vogue. White embroidery on linen has a frigid and monotonous aspect: that with coloured threads is more vivacious in effect, but by frequent washings the colour gets fainter and fainter until it almost disappears. But white embroidery, relieved by open spaces in, or shapes cut from, the linen ground, is possessed of an altogether new charm; and from a sense of this the birth may be traced of an art in the results of which happy contrasts are effected between ornamental details of close texture and others of open work.

Fig. 84.—Linen band ornamented with embroideries in white thread and parts of cutwork, sixteenth century (Bonnaffé collection).

Of this character is cutwork embroidery, or cutting
out certain selected spaces from between the devices

Fig 85.—Embroidery of drawn threadwork (*Musée des Arts
décoratifs*, from a design published in 1588).

embroidered on the linen.   Such cut spaces filled in with
open devices (*à jours*) were at first sparingly adopted

(fig. 84) ; but by degrees, as the pleasant effects ensuing from the use of them were appreciated, they were more extensively employed (figs. 83 and 88). Sometimes the flower or other ornament would be worked on the linen and edged with stitching of the button-hole class, and adjoining it corresponding devices would be wrought with the needle in the middle of empty spaces cut out of the linen (see fig. 84). Thus cutwork as a title is applicable to specimens of varied ornamental effect ; and although the principle of the process remains the same in all, it is distinctively a class of embroidery upon a material and comes within the definition given in chap. i., p. 9, of this book.

Drawn thread embroidery was another cognate work. For this certain threads would be drawn out from the linen ground, and others left, upon and between which needlework was made. With Turkish women this class of embroidery seems to have been a very favourite pastime, and is still much affected in harems at Constantinople ; its employment in the East dates from very early times * (figs. 85 and 86).

Contemporary with these drawn threadworks were embroideries of similar effect, in which the skill in

---

* Withdrawing threads from a fabric is perhaps referred to in the ollowing quotation from Lucan's *Pharsalia*, book x., ver. 142 :—

> " *Candida Sidonio perlucent pectora filo,*
> *Quod Nilotis acus compressum pectine Serum,*
> *Solvit, et extenso laxavit stamina velo.*"

" Her white breasts shine through the Sidonian fabric, which pressed down with the comb (or sley) of the Seres, the needle of the Nile workman has separated, and has loosened the warp by stretching out (or withdrawing) the weft," p. 5, *Descriptive Catalogue of the Collections of Tapestry and Embroidery in the South Kensington Museum.*

needlework was almost entirely devoted to working over the threads left to form the interstices or open reticulations about the pattern ; or else to taking stitches so as to convey the impression of a reticulated ground about the pattern which was left on the linen (fig. 87).

From the first of the two just-mentioned methods sprang the idea that instead of laboriously withdrawing threads from stout linen it would be more convenient to introduce a needle-made pattern into

an open reticulated ground, a "quintain," as it was termed, after the name of a little town in Brittany, a district famous in the Middle Ages for its linens. The reticulations or meshes of these "quintains" were made more and more open, so that at length many of these

Fig. 86.—Design for a drawn threadwork (belonging to Madame Franck).

special fabrics were nothing more than nets. Such nets go by the name of "*lacis*" in France. "*Lacis*," according to the *Dictionnaire Antique de Furretière*, published in 1684, "is a sort of thread or silk formed into a tissue of net or *réseuil*, the threads of which were knotted or interlaced the one into the other."

Embroidery was done upon the *lacis* by darning or running threads into a certain number of meshes ; the monotony of the open meshes forming the ground about

Fig. 87.—Short-stitch embroidery on linen, the ornament being left in the linen, in the character of patterns usually done in drawn thread-work, sixteenth century (*Musée des Arts décoratifs*).

the pattern, would sometimes be broken by working

into them little delicate devices such as stars or crossed diagonals, or making little loops or picots upon their threads. This darning work was easy of execution;

and, the stitches being regulated by counting the meshes, effective geometric shapes could be produced; less skilful embroiderers excelled in this more than in the drawn threadwork. Small squares of *lacis* could be worked separately, and this characteristic of the process found much favour with women, who applied themselves to making all sorts of textile ornaments for religious and secular use. Altar cloths and baptismal napkins, as well as bed coverlets and table-cloths, were decorated with these squares of net embroidery, inserted most often into larger squares of plain linen, which again might be picked out here and there with little cut points.[*]

Fig. 88.—Sampler with squares of cutwork (*Musée des Arts décoratifs*).

Many specimens of such embroideries are extant.

A linen cap, ornamented with cutwork and very finely wrought white thread embroidery, in which

---

[*] This combination of open embroideries was called "*Punto reale*" or Royal point, by some of the Italian designers (see *Pattern Book*, by Parasole, 1616).

appear eagles, is in the Cluny Museum, and is said
to have belonged to Charles V.

In linen bands embroidered like that in fig. 84,
personages are sometimes figured in the open cut out
spaces.

An alb, said to be the work of Anne of Bohemia
(1527), is preserved in the cathedral at Prague, and is
of linen drawn-threadwork.

Punto a redexelo, embroidery upon open reticulated
ground, is mentioned in the deed, dated 1493, appor-
tioning various articles between the sisters Angelo and
Ippolita Sforza-Visconti of Milan, a document to which
we shall have occasion to make several references.

Catherine de Médicis had a bed draped with squares
of *réseuil* or *lacis*, and it is recorded that " the girls and
servants of her household consumed much time in
making squares of *réseuil*." What she possessed in
the way of squares of embroidered net is incredible ;
the inventory of her property and goods includes a
coffer containing three hundred and eighty-one of such
squares, unmounted, whilst in another were found five
hundred and thirty-eight squares, some worked with
rosettes or with blossoms, and others with nosegays.*

At a very slightly later date, lengths of insertions
made of darned or run net (*lacis*) were used, and of
such there are good specimens in the *Musée des Arts
décoratifs* (fig. 89).

Part of a handsome curtain border of darned net,
with numerous personages, amongst whom is a hunter,
is shown in fig. 91.

At the opening of the sixteenth century we have

* *Inventory of Catherine de Médicis*, by Bonnaffé.

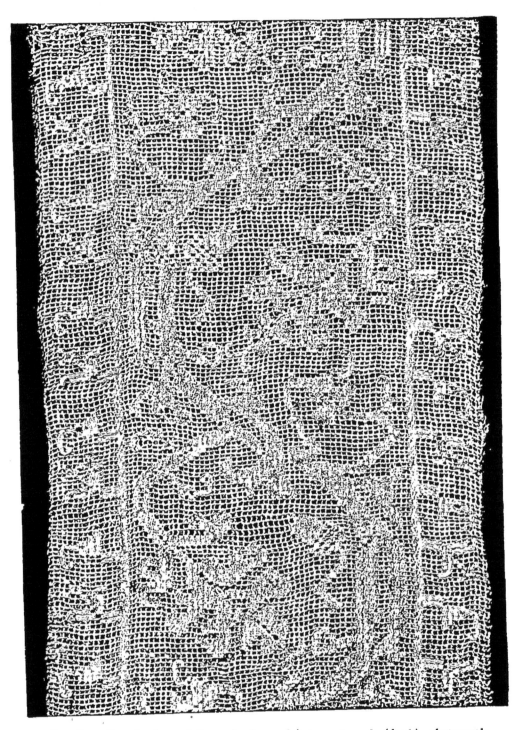

Fig. 89.—Band of stout threads darned into network (*lacis*), sixteenth century (*Musée des Arts décoratifs*).

white thread embroideries on linen, cut points, and drawn threadwork, followed by needlework upon quintain or open canvas, and lastly by darning or running upon net or *lacis*.

Fig. 90.—Italian design taken from Cesare Vecellio's *Corona delle virtuose donne*.

Pattern books.—Now, during the early development of these open ground embroideries, some difficulty was experienced in procuring patterns for them. Such as could be drawn by pen upon parchment, or made into

needlework samplers on bits of linen, were passed from
hand to hand.   This was soon found to be tedious and

Fig. 91.—Curtain border of darned net (*lacis*), French work
of the sixteenth century.

insufficient to satisfy a demand, the sources of which
multiplied with rapidity.

The assistance which embroiderers derived from

the art of engraving and various modes of printing has already been alluded to. Printers of books became numerous, first in the Rhenish countries, and subsequently in France, Italy, and elsewhere.

The plan, of reproducing and publishing gleanings of different and well-contrived patterns for embroidery with open grounds, seems to have been first taken advantage of by Pierre Quinty of Cologne.

In 1527 he published his " New and Subtle Book concerning the Art and Science of Embroidery, Fringes, Tapestry-making, as well as of other Crafts done with the Needle." This work passed through many editions.* The first is in French, but succeeding ones are in German, signed Quintell instead of Quinty, and contain a portrait of Charles V. All the designs are for embroidery and not for lace. This is also the case with an identical reprint of patterns issued by Vostermans, published at Antwerp, with English letterpress.

The successive issues of new pattern books made by French, Italian, and other publishers supply one with a means of tracing the stages in the transition from white thread embroidery to needlepoint lace. With those for squares and bands of *lacis*, patterns for indented or vandyke borders or edgings, involving new departures in execution, gradually appear. And we now meet with a style of needlework which differs from embroidery in not being wrought upon a stuff foundation. As the

---

* For further details as to pattern books, see the appendix to Mrs. Bury-Palliser's *History of Lace*, and articles by Girolamo d'Adda in the *Gazette des Beaux Arts*, 1863-64, and those by Duplessis in the *Revue des Arts décoratifs*, 1887.

dentations and vandykes become more and more elaborated with open devices, so the needlework for them assumes the phase of embroidery, without apparent foundation whatever, done as it were "in the air." We thus find ourselves confronted with the newly evolved lace, which in a few years and by rapid strides specializes itself in an immense variety of patterns and subtleties of stitchery.

A new fashion arose amongst men and women in Italy for decking their necks with fluted or pleated collars called ruffs. The connections formed by the Médicis with families of the French court introduced this Italian fashion, which soon spread over Europe. But it was hardly one of common sense and convenience, for the most fashionable ruffs were made of grotesque sizes. Contemporary writers, referring to them, speak of them as "gadrooned like organ pipes, contorted or crinkled like cabbages, and as big as the sails of a windmill."

Poets satirized these absurd collars in passages similar to the following, taken from the *Vertus et propriétés des Mignons* in 1576 :—

> "*Le col ne se tourne à leur aise*
> *Dans le long reply de leur fraise.*"*

---

* "The most curious wives," says Stowe, "now made themselves ruffs of cambric, and sent them to Madame Dinghan to be starched, who charged high prices. After a time they made themselves ruffs of lawn, and thereupon arose a general scoff or byword that shortly they would make their ruffs of spiders' webs." Stowe in another passage writes, "Both men and women wore them intolerably large, being a quarter of a yard deep, and twelve lengths in a ruff." In London this fashion was termed the "French ruff"; in France, on the other hand, it was the "English monster."—MRS. BURY-PALLISER's *History of Lace.*

But what chiefly interests us in the matter is that a fashion had been created which stimulated the use of a large quantity of laces, as trimming borders for ruffs and their companion cuffs or sleeves.

During this period ladies' dresses and nobles' doublets were enriched with lace insertions, interlacing designs for which are to be seen in the majority of the pattern books we are now about to examine.

Those by Antonio Tagliente (1528) and Nicolo d'Aristotile (1530) are the earliest published in Venice. They are interesting, not solely on account of their patterns, but also because the introductory text to them gives us insight into the different methods of needle-work, stitches, etc., then used in Italy. Tagliente entitles this first book, "Samples for Embroidery" (*Esempio di Ricami*). He states that his patterns may be wrought in thread and in silk, "*sete di varii colori*," also "*con argento i oro tirato*," with silver and gold wire or thread. He enumerates amongst the stitches in which his patterns may be worked, "*disfilato*," drawn threads; "*fatto sur la rete*," work on net-ground, "*a magliete*," of small meshes; "*punto damaschino*," damask stitch; "*rilevato*," raised work; "*filo supra punto*," darning; "*croceato*," cross stitch; "*punto tagliato*, cut point; and, lastly, "*punto in aere*," point in the air, a term, as we shall see, which was henceforward descriptive of needlepoint lace in Italy. Notwithstanding that he named his book "Samples for Embroidery," Tagliente seemed to be acquainted with the specialty known as *punto in aere*, as patterns for its earlier productions are included by name at least in his work.

He further is careful to specify the purposes to which

the different embroideries may be put ; for men's and women's collars, for "*camisciole con pettorali*," shirts or chemises with embroidered fronts, for "*frisi di contorni di letti*," bed vallances ; and for "*entemelle di cuscini*," insertions on pillowcases.

Here, then, we have instances of ornamental needle-work, the immediate ancestor of needlepoint lace, in its application to costume and articles of furniture.

Nicolo d'Aristotile inscribes his book to ladies and young girls, *fanciulle*, who will learn from it how to "*lavorare, cusire, ricamare i far tutte quelle gentilleze que una dona virtuosa podra far con l'aco in mano*," to work, sew, embroider, and do all the fancy work that a virtuous woman can with a needle in her hand.

To this end his compilation consists of old and new patterns, and its title is *Gli Universali dei Belle Ricami Antichi e Moderni* ("The Universality of Fine Ancient and Modern Embroideries ").

The foregoing suggests that, prior to the books just noticed, others had been produced, or, at least, that there were early drawings of patterns which publishers utilized and developed. Tagliente writes that he himself designed "*con studio continuo et vigilante cura*," with continuous study and vigilant care, a large part of his book, the remainder of which is made up of "*varii disegni di maestri copiuti*," different designs copied from the masters.

The existence of drawn patterns and worked samplers is attested by various documents, etc.

The inventory of Edward VI., King of England (1552), contains the entry of a parchment book with a variety of patterns :—

Item: (Sampler) or set of patterns worked on Normandy canvas, with green and black silks. These may possibly have been used by the king's sisters.

In the preface of the first of his books, known to us, Vavassore writes, "*Havedo io pel passato fatto alcuni libri di esempli,*" having myself produced some time ago a few books of patterns.

This Giovanni Antonio Vavassore, reputed to have been a pupil of Mantegna, and known amongst engravers under the name of Zoan Andrea, pilfered in the most shameless manner from the works of other publishers, and was accordingly dubbed Guadagnino, the Rapacious. His first work, *l'Esemplario di Lavori* (1530), reproduces designs of German embroideries with double-headed eagles and other *motifs* of anything but an Italian character. During the course of twenty-five years he issued innumerable impressions and editions of his patterns, heading the series with the pompous titles so much affected by the Italian pattern-book publishers; at one time it is *Fontana de gli Esempli* ("The Fountain of Patterns"), 1546; *La Fior de gli Esempli* ("The Flower of Patterns"); *La Corona di Ricami* ("The Crown of Embroideries"), 1550. He takes credit to himself that the authors of other similar books have not known, as he has, how to count stitches, "*numerar li punti,*" and that, consequently, the ladies have been left without guide as to the way in which the patterns were to be worked, "*le donne noli possino meter in opera.*"

But Venice was not the only publishing centre for open stitched patterns. Francisque Pelegrin, styled "*noble home de Florence,*" printed his "*Fleur de Science de Pourtraicture et Patrons de Broderie Façon Arabique et Ytalique*," in France, securing the sanction of the king, Francis I., thereto, on the " 17th day of June, in the year 1530, and sixteenth of our reign."

Thus the name of Francis I. is connected with this work of Francisque Pelegrin, as Charles V.'s is with that of Quintell, an instance of the simultaneous encouragement bestowed by two rival courts upon needlework and pattern books to propagate its practice.

It is, moreover, interesting from the point of view of style in pattern to note the two currents of supply for pattern publishers, the one coming from the North and the other from Italy.

Embroideries upon open grounds, done by counted stitches, are almost entirely of a German character. Their patterns are principally composed of eagles, and heraldic emblems, oak leaves, acorns, holly and thistles, all of which belong to Northern vegetation ; and, lastly, of hunting scenes, designed with a remarkable air of truth.

The *motifs* in Italian needleworks which were largely of cut points, and *punti in aere*, points in the air, consist on the other hand, of oleander blossoms, and elegant wreaths and scrolls, conventional foliage of the acanthus type, figures of people real or imaginary, standing under arcades or separated by columns, vases, and fountains ; and very often musical instruments are introduced (fig. 90). Besides these, *paesi con historie antiche*, landscapes with mythological scenes play an important part ; saints are at times alternated with Olympian gods ; and hunting episodes, less realistic than the Northern ones, are pictured with fauns, and nymphs

or *amorini* shooting arrows. In French and German
patterns lifelike huntsmen wind their hunting horns,
and chase boars (fig. 91).

That the publishers were not the designers of the
patterns may be inferred from the fact that in a set of
collected designs, Italian, French, Flemish, English, and
even those of the *façon arabique* (Saracenic style), were
heterogeneously mixed together.

In 1543, fifteen years after the books by Tagliente
and d'Aristotile had been issued, Rob. Mathio Pagan
published at Venice his *Giardinetto novi di punti tagliati
i gropposi*, or "New Garden of cut and knotted Points."
These are for cut linen embroideries, or embroideries
upon open linen, or net, but with more relief imparted to them than earlier ones. This relief was
obtained by knotted stitches "*gropposi.*" The *motifs*
of the patterns are "*à fogliami,*" of foliage as well as
"*in storia*" of episodes. A little later, in his edition
of 1558, entitled *La Gloria di Punti* ("The Glory of
Stitches"), he adds *li punti in aere*, points in the air, of
which he had not spoken previously. His book in its
two editions thus displays the transition from embroidery
with open stitches to needlepoint lace with raised work.

A certain number of these pattern books bear no
authors' names, and some are undated ; these are therefore only classifiable by analogy with those of which
the authors and dates are known. One of the most
interesting of them is *Le Pompe*, dated 1558, author
unknown. Many were produced by friars or monks, as,
for instance, the *Triompho di Lavori a Fogliami* ("The
Triumph of Foliated Work"), by Fra Hieronimo of Padua,
in 1555, and that by Antoine Belin, recluse of St. Martial

at Lyons, who co-operated with Jehan Mayol, Carmelite monk at Lyons. The publisher of the last-named book was Pierre de St. Lucie dit Le Prince. On the title-page is a cut of women instructing children in needlework. Monks probably designed such books for purposes of instruction ; for use as class-books, in fact.

The same sort of remark applies to a large number of patterns brought together and published under the direction of women, the designs of which have great individuality. Dame Isabetta-Catanea Parasole brought out a book in 1594, at Venice, an issue of which she repeated the next year at Rome, entitled *Specchio delle Virtuose Done* (" The Mirror of Virtuous Women "). The drawing of the patterns proclaims the practised hand of a workwoman thoroughly conversant with the *punti in aria*, needlepoint laces, and the *punti a piombini*, bobbin laces.

Another woman (Lucrezia Romana) to some extent influenced Venetian wood engravers. Mathio Pagan dedicated his *Giardinetto di Punti* (" Garden of the Stitches ") to her ; and on one of the pages of Giovanni Ostans' pattern book (fig. 92) is a woodcut, in which she is represented surrounded by a group of women, whose work she is directing.

In 1584 Dominique de Sera, an Italian, follows the example of Francisque Pellegrin, by publishing a set of patterns at Paris, called *Livre de Lingerie*, for instruction in the noble and gentle art of the needle (*de l'esguille*) according to the methods he saw " in Italy, Spain, Roumania, Germany, and other countries." But, fearing that this may be insufficient attraction for French patrons, he adds " several patterns designed by Jean

Cousin, painter at Paris," youthful works of one who subsequently ranked amongst the most illustrious of French artists.

Queen Catherine de Médicis, wife of Henry II., and mother of Charles IX., induced one Federic Vinciolo to come from Italy and make ruffs and gadrooned collars, the fashion of which she started in France. According to Brantôme she gave him the sole right, for many years, of selling such articles.

This encouraged the said Vinciolo to collect a number of patterns specially suitable for the trimmings of these ruffs. Under the patronage of Louise de Lorraine, wife of Henry III., who succeeded Charles IX., Vinciolo published the completest known series

Fig. 92.—Design from pattern book by Giovanni Ostans.

of patterns. Its first part is dated 1587; the title is as follows:—

"The singular and new designs (*pourtraicts*) and work for linen (*lingerie*) for use as patterns for all sorts of stitches, cutwork, *lacis*, and others. Dedicated to the Queen. Newly invented, to the profit and content of noble ladies and young ladies, and other gentle spirits, *amateurs* of such art.   By the Seigneur Federic de Vinciolo, Venetian.   In Paris at Jean Le Clerc the younger, Rue Chartière, St. Denis, 1587.   With the sanction of the King."   On the last page of the work is : "Sanction granted for nine years to Jean Le Clerc the younger, dealer in storybooks at Paris, signed the 27th June, 1587.   From the printing press of David Le Clerc, Rue Frementel, at the sign of the Golden star : in 4to."

For twenty years, at least, new editions of the *Singuliers Pourtraicts* appeared without intermission; and each succeeding edition contained a few new additional plates.

Vinciolo, who dedicated them to the Queen with multitudinous compliments in prose and verse, adds in his inflated style: "I have greatly desired, honourable readers, to place before you, for works of a magnificent standard, the present designs, which I have kept back hidden and unknown until now, when I offer them with a cheerful heart to the French nation !"

All, however, are not entirely invented by himself, since he owns to "having obtained from Italy certain rare and singular patterns, and having originated a few to the best of my poor powers." . . .   Still he asserts his superiority over all his predecessors in the art, by stating patronizingly that "he is assured that those patterns, less perfected and more rudely outlined, have already served and been of some profit."   Although Vavassore had counted and numbered stitches (*numerare li punti*) before him, Vinciolo does the same in his third edition, and placidly states it to have been "never before seen or thought of."   After which, one cannot resist smiling at his saying, "I think, friend reader, that you will not ignore in any way the great and sedulous labour I must have expended in drawing and giving light to the larger quantity of most excellent patterns for needlework contained in this present book."

We will not prolong our remarks upon these pattern books;* as we turn over the leaves of many of them it is not difficult to identify most with the period of the Médicis and to recognize the widespread influence of Italian taste in the publications of other countries. Venice, moreover, asserts its supremacy in producing fine laces, and drives a considerable trade in collars and cuffs, worn as frequently by men as by women of quality.

Perhaps the oldest painting in which lace is depicted is that of a portrait of a lady by Carpaccio, who died about 1523. It is in the academy at Venice. The cuffs of the lady are edged with a narrow lace, the pattern of which reappears in Vecellio's *Corona*, not published until 1591; this particular pattern was therefore in use

---

* It will suffice here to note that the better-known pattern books, esides those already named are—1534, Johan Schwartzemberger, Augsburg; 1546, Gormont, Paris; 1554, Balthazar Sylvius or Dubois, Paris; 1560, Christofer Froschowern, Zurich; 1593, Jeromino Calepino, Venice; 1564, Ve. Jean Ruelle, Paris; 1568, Nicolas Basseus (four editions), Frankfurt; 1591, J. Woolff, London; 1591, Cesare Vecellio (nine editions), Venice (fig. 90); 1597, Jeande Glen, Liège, 1597, Balthazar Laimoxen, Nuremberg; 1598, Jacques Foillet, Montbéliard; 1661, Johan Sibmacher, Nuremberg; 1604, Paul Tozzi, Padua; 1605, The Englishman Mignerak, Paris.

Interesting reproductions of many of these books have been recently made by F. Ongania of Venice, and other foreign publishers; in France by Hippolyte Cocheris, Emmanuel Bocher, Madame Veuve Perrault & Son, and Armand Durand.

at least eighty years before it got into circulation with other published patterns.

Of similar date, no doubt, were the "ancient laces" mentioned in an inventory, dated 1598, which furbished the bed of J. Bta. Valier, bishop of Cividale di Belluno.

Notwithstanding the success which attended the first appearance of Venetian laces, they met with opposition even in their own country; for officers of the Republic, the *Proveditori alle Pompe*, issued several ordinances against the wearing of *punti in aere* in towns, under pain of a fine of two hundred ducats. One of these sumptuary laws passed in 1514 lays down the limits of fashion in "ladies' cloaks, laces, gloves embroidered with gold and silk, embroideries generally, fans, gondolas, and sedan chairs." *

However, on the occasion of the French king's (Henry III.) passing through Venice in 1574, special leave was granted to ladies to wear all sorts of costume, ornaments, and jewellery whatsoever, "even such as were prohibited by the ordinances."

Henry III. certainly brought back with him on his return from this journey a lively taste for all sorts of Italian affectations to which his mother Catherine de Médicis had accustomed him from his childhood. And we hear of him being so punctilious over his ruffs, that he would set himself to iron and goffer his cuffs and collars rather than see their pleats and gadroons limp and out of shape.† This probably explains why Vinciolo, in dedicating his patterns to the

---

* *Venice*, by Charles Yriarte, p. 222.
† Charles Blanc, *L'Art dans la Parure*, p. 297.

Queen, did not forget, in sly courtier manner, to add a portrait of the King who gave so much heed to his laces.

Summary.—These detailed explanations seemed necessary with the view of giving some insight into the transition from white embroideries to laces: they indicate that in the sixteenth century no laces beyond the *punti in aere* were really known, although these were used in bands of insertion and for edgings of dentated shapes. The close portions of the *motifs* and floral devices in such *punti* were worked in a filling-in stitch, lightened with small holes arranged like veins in a leaf, or ornamentally grouped together ; the contours of these close-worked devices were rarely outlined with a thread ; and the portions, when rendered in relief, were worked with a knotted stitch. More elegant effects were obtained by means of small loopings or purls cast upon the edges of some of the details, with charming effect.

In conclusion it may be said that needlepoint lace of this period is found to be so closely allied with embroidery in cut or drawn-thread work, or embroidery on *lacis* (net), and other needlework wrought with open grounds, that it seems to be merely a slight variety of one or the other of them. It is not until the succeeding century that it acquires a really independent character and individuality.

CHAPTER II.

*THE SEVENTEENTH CENTURY—VENETIAN POINTS—
MARKED INFLUENCE OF LOUIS XIV. AND COLBERT
—POINT DE FRANCE.*

To properly follow the course of, and deviations, in
lace-making it is necessary to study costume from the
sixteenth century to our time. This at least is the advice
given by M. G. Duplessis in his remarkable articles
entitled " *Indications sommaires sur les documents utiles
aux artistes industriels dans le département des estampes
à la Bibliothèque nationale.** One result of his researches
deserves our special attention. He finds distinct
evidence that the production of the more noteworthy
of earlier laces owes more to the influence of men
than to that of women. When men adopted the
fashion of wearing laces, designs for them become of
a distinctively artistic character. Man readily criticizes
the adornments of the opposite sex, and cannot therefore but feel flattered in nowadays reviving the remembrance that the costliest productions of the art
of lace-making originated under his direct influence,
whether he exercised it for the enrichment of his courtly
costume as a great noble or for that of his alb and rochet
as a prelate.

* See two articles by M. G. Duplessis (director of the *Département
des Estampes* in the Bibliothèque *Nationale*) in the *Revue des Arts
décoratifs* for February and March, 1887.

Ruffs and their companion cuffs, says Quicherat made their first appearance as articles of costume about 1540.* At this time needlework for the *punti in aere* also is first practised, and designers begin to relax the geometric character of their devices and to enter upon a freer and more wealthy style of pattern for the *punti a fogliami*.

The spirit of Flemish and Dutch painters, great lovers of flowers, readily infuses itself into this period of pattern-making, and is as speedily apparent in Italy as in France. Under Henry IV. (1589—1610) and Louis XIII. (1610—1643) pleated and gadrooned ruffs disappear and are replaced by wide flat collars of Dutch linen, garnished with laces falling over the shoulders of men or perked up fan-fashion at the back of women's heads. The shapes still retain the ornamentation imparted to insertions and trimming borders, *bandes et passements;* but the dentations of the borders are less pointed than under the Valois. The well-balanced scallop forms are finely curved, and give rise to the employment of other than geometric *motifs.* Expanding tulips come into vogue as ornamental devices, and remind us of the costly extravagances of Dutch tulip fanciers. Nothing so completely conveys an idea of the style which collars assume at this time as the engravings by Abraham Bosse. "There is hardly a specimen of Abraham Bosse's work," writes Quicherat, "which does not display the forms of collars, frills (*jabots*), or cuffs." Fig. 95 shows us a lace shop in the "Gallery of the Palace," decked out with its wares, and provides us with incontrovertible authority for the

* Quicherat, *Histoire de Costume en France.*

Fig. 95.—Lace shop in the *Galerie du Palais*
(after Abraham Bosse).

style of laces then in use. Everything in the embellish-

ment of male attire of the time lends itself to enrichment by means of laces. Great collars, cuffs turned
back, gloves, doublets, breeches, and even boots are all
profusely trimmed.

Bits of furniture are literally enveloped with *lacis*
work or laces, especially beds ; head and foot-boards,
canopies and their supporting pillars, are completely
hidden beneath these cloudy fabrics ; from the corners
of the canopies spring plumes reaching to the ceiling,
and all below them is a pendent mass of lacy draperies.

The inventory of Charles de Bourbon, 1613, and
that of his wife, Countess of Soissons, 1644, includes
mention of a bed decked with "a pavilion of linen
hangings, with bands of net made up of squares, the
head-board covered with similar material, the inside of
the canopy, the covers for the pillars, three curtains
and a head curtain, a sheet of similar linen with a band
of *réseuil*, a state coverlet, all bordered with lace." . . .

Laces, too, were used as trimmings for the interiors,
and along the great open window-sashes, of coaches and
carriages, which increased in number as well made royal
roads superseded the badly kept highways of the Middle
Ages.

These exaggerated uses of lace, etc., vexed Henry IV.
very much. For all that, however, he was a good and
patient prince, anxious to see progress made with the
industries of his country. In 1607 he called the Royal
Tapestry Manufactory into being. Previously, in 1598,
he had had planted in the Bois de Boulogne fifteen
thousand mulberry trees which had been brought from
Milan by one Balbani, and were put under the charge
of Olivier de Serres. At the chateau de Madrid close

at hand the king had established a silk-worm nursery ;
but the austere disposition of Huguenot Sully, the

Fig. 94.—A dandy discarding his laces (after Abraham Bosse).

king's first minister, did not harmonize with such pre-
occupations. "You want iron and soldiers," said he

to his master, "and not laces and silks to trick out fops !"

In the face of absurd abuses through which certain nobles ruined themselves, Henry IV. felt compelled to issue a few sumptuary edicts intended to lessen them.

Louis XIII., with his religious rigour in striking contrast with Henry IV.'s geniality, was much more severe, and promulgated in 1629 the edict already referred to, under the title of " Regulation as to Super-fluity in Costume." Draconic as this law appeared, its application was not rigidly enforced, and people did not dissemble their contempt for it. Many of Abraham Bosse's engravings cheerfully caricature the supposed effects of this law, and the first series of them were extremely popular. The same subject was used by him for three distinct versions of the " Courtier obeying the last edict," in which a gentleman is represented pulling off his collar, cuffs, and the minor elegancies of his court dress, throwing them on to a chair, and re-clothing himself in simple attire, so little trimmed that he presents a comparatively sorry appearance after the transformation (fig. 94). His *valet de chambre* is about to lock up the laced clothes. Beneath him are the lines :—

> *C'est avec regret que mon matire*
> *Quitte ces beaux habillemens*
> *Semés de riches passemens*
> *Qui le fesoient si bien paroistre.*
> *Mais, d'un autre côté, je pense*
> *Qu'étant avare comme il est,*
> *Asseurément l'édit luy plaist,*
> *Pour ce qu'il règle la dépense.*

Je vais donc mettre dans le coffre
Tous ces vêtemens superflus,
Et quoiqu'il ne les porte plus,
*Je ne crains pas qu'il me les offre.**

Fig. 95 displays us the lady inconsolably dressing herself in clothes without laces :—

Quoique j'aye assez de beauté
Pour asseurer sans vanité
Qu'il n'est point de femme plus belle,
Il semble pourtant, à mes yeux,
Qu'avec de l'or et la dentelle,
Je m'ajuste encore bien mieux.†

The king's severity against the prodigalities of courtiers is nevertheless justified when one finds, for example, that Cinq Mars left at his death in 1642 more than three hundred sets of collars and cuffs trimmed with lace !

At the end of Louis XIII.'s reign, lace-making had become an industry quite distinct from that of embroidery. Embroidery with open stitches and upon nets was still slightly practised; but active and special centres were organized for the pursuit of the novel and charming industry of lace-making, the origin of which and its admission into the confederation of the industrial arts do not reach back into fabulous ages; from its

---

* It is with regret that my master doffs the fine clothes covered with trimmings, which gave him such a handsome appearance. On the other hand, I think, that being a niggard as he is, the edict must surely please him, so far as it affects his expenses. I go then and put all these superfluous garments in the cupboard, and as he will wear them no more, I shall not fear he will give them to me.

† In spite of my personal beauty which, without vanity, cannot be surpassed by that of another woman, it still seems to my eyes that with gold and laces I further enhance my charms.

commencement it at once took a position of the first
rank in industrial arts.

Fig. 95.—A lady of fashion discarding her laces (after Abraham
Bosse).

Moreover, at this moment there succeeded to the
throne of France a young king whose influence in

developing the new-born industry was decisive; it may
be safely said that the sixty-eight years of his reign witnessed the production of the most stately needlepoint
laces; the transformation of Venetian point, and the
outburst of *Points d'Alençon, d'Argentan, de Bruxelles,
d'Angleterre*, occur during this period of the Grand
Monarque, which, in respect of many of these laces,
covers both those of their birth and apogee.

Nevertheless, at the commencement of the vogue for
laces, under the regency of the queen-mother, Anne
of Austria, they were objects of divers sumptuary
edicts.

One issued during the last year of Mazarin, 1660,
kindled very great anxiety, its publication taking place
on the eve of the young king's marriage. Everybody
had had their gala dresses trimmed with braids,
guipures, and fine laces, in honour of the arrival of the
bride, and so the cruelty of the edict was doubly felt.
On all sides murmurs arose to such a degree that
Moliére, at the risk of giving offence to the king, endeavoured to mollify public discontent by a mock eulogy
of the decree which he introduced into the *École des
Maris*.

> *Oh ! trois et quatre fois béni soit cet édit*
> *Par qui des vêtements le luxe est interdit !*
> *Les peines des maris ne seront plus si grandes*
> *Et les femmes auront un frein à leurs demandes.*
> *Oh ! que je sais au roi bon gré de ces décris,*
> *Et que, pour le repos de ces mêmes maris,*
> *Je voudrais bien qu'on fit de la coquetterie*
> *Comme de la guipure et de la broderie.*

The edict of 1660 provoked a clique of fashionable
dames, who used to meet at the Hotel de Rambouillet,

to compose a set of satirical verses, the mere technical interest of which is so conspicuous that it cannot be passed by in silence, as every then known lace is mentioned in it. It is entitled *La Révolte des Passements.* No author's name is given, but the verses are dedicated to Mademoiselle de la Trousse, a cousin of Madame de Sévigné. Mrs. Bury-Palliser has in her book on the *History of Lace* made an excellent *resumé* of these verses, and we extract it in full.

" In consequence of the sumptuary edict against luxury in apparel Mesdames les Broderies,—

> " *Les Poincts, Dentelles, Passemens,*
> *Qui, par une vaine despence,*
> *Ruinoient aujourd'hui la France—*

meet and concert measures for their common safety. *Point de Gênes*, with *Point de Raguse*, first address the company. Next, *Point de Venise*, who seems to look on *Point de Raguse* with a jealous eye, exclaims,—

> " *Encor pour vous, Poinct de Raguse,*
> *Il est bon, crainte d'attentat,*
> *D'en vouloir purger un Estat.*
> *Les gens aussi fins que vous êtes*
> *Ne sont bons que, comme vous faites,*
> *Pour ruiner tous les Estats.*
> *Et nous, Aurillac et Venise*
> *Si nous plions notre valise,*

what will be our fate ?

" The other laces speak in their turn, most despondently, till a ' *Veille broderie d'or,*' consoling them, talks of the vanity of this world : ' Who knows it better than I, who have dwelt in kings' houses ?' One ' *grande dentelle d'Angleterre* ' now proposes they should all retire to a convent. To this the ' *Dentelles de Flandres'* object. They would sooner be sewn at once to the bottom of a petticoat.

"Mesdames les Broderies resign themselves to become '*ameublements*,' the more devout of the party to appear as '*devants d'autels*.' Those who feel too young to renounce the world and its vanities will seek refuge in the masquerade shops.

"'*Dentelle noire d'Angleterre*' lets herself out cheap to a fowler, as a net to catch woodcocks, for which she felt '*assez propre*' in her present predicament.

"The Points all resolve to retire to their own countries save Aurillac, who fears she may be turned into a strainer '*pour passer les fromages d'Auvergne*,' a smell insupportable to one who had revelled in civet and orange-flower.

"All were starting

> "*Chacun, dissimulant sa rage,*
> *Doucement ployoit son bagage,*
> *Résolu d'obéir au sort.*

when

> "*Une pauvre très malheureuse,*
> *Qu'on appelle, dit-on, la Gueuse,*

arrives, in a great rage, from a village in the environs of Paris. She is not of high birth, but has her feelings all the same. She has no refuge, not even a place in the hospital. Let them follow her advice, and '*elle engageoit sa chainette*,' she will replace them all in their former position.

"Next morn the Points assemble. '*Une grande cravate fanfaron*' exclaims,—

> "*Il nous faut venger cet affront;*
> *Révoltons-nous noble assemblée.*

" A council of war ensues.

> " *Là-dessus, le Point d'Alençon,*
> *Ayant bien appris sa leçon,*
> *Fit une fort belle harangue.*

" Flanders now boasts how she had made two campaigns under Monsieur as a cravat, another had learned the art of war under Turenne, a third was torn at the siege of Dunkirk.

> " *Racontant des combats qu'ils ne virent jamais,*

one and all had figured at some siege or battle.

> " *Qu'avons à redouter?*

cries *Dentelle d'Angleterre.* Not so, thinks *Point de Gênes,* ' *qui avait le corps un peu gros.'*

" They all swear,

> " *Foy de Passement*
> *Foy de Poincts et de Broderie,*
> *De Guipure et d'Orfévrerie*
> *De Gueuse de toute façon,*

to declare open war and to banish Parliament.

" The Laces assemble at the fair of St. Germain, there to be reviewed by *General Luxe.*

" The muster-roll is called over by Colonel *Sotte Dépense. Dentelles de Moresse, Escadrons de Neige, Dentelles de Hâvre, Escrues, Soies Noires,* and *Points d'Espagnes,* etc., march forth in warlike array, to conquer or to die. At the first approach of the artillery they all take to their heels, and are condemned by a council of war, the Points to be made into tinder for the sole use of the king's musquetaires, the Laces to be converted into paper, the *Dentelles, Escrues, Gueuses, Passemens,* and silk lace to be made into cordage and sent to the galleys, the Gold and

Silver Laces, the original authors of the sedition, to be burned alive.

"Finally, through the intercession of Love,

"*Le petit dieu plein de finesse,*

they are again pardoned and restored to court favour."

The poem is of the highest value to us, in its enumeration of the laces in use in 1661, and in its pourtrayal of the character peculiar to each.

From amongst the names thus given we select two for special note in connection with needlepoint laces. These are the *Point de Raguse* and the *Point de Venise*. The investigation of the origin of the great transformation which was taking place in patterns of Venetian laces leads us to inquire if the rivalry between the two towns, as set forth in the poem, may not point to a suggestion that the rich foliated scroll patterns possessing Oriental character, were first designed in Ragusa, before Venice adopted kindred works. Venice, as Queen of the Adriatic, shared her power with no other place; still, the poem certainly seems to say that Ragusa had made even finer laces than Venice, as—

Les gens aussi fins que vous êtes,
Ne sont bons que, comme vous faites,
*Pour ruiner tous les Éstats.**

But, Ragusa being so effectually beaten out of the field, in the matter of laces, by Venice, no means are really left us for determining the exact character of the Points de Raguse apparently so highly esteemed by the clique of the hotel de Rambouillet.†

* "The people (Venetians), as skilled as you (of Ragusa) are, are only useful, as you are, to ruin all estates."

† Ragusa is comparatively near the Montenegrin seaboard, and north-western coast of Greece, and in the fifteenth and early six-

However this may be, Venice certainly monopolized the production of, and commerce in, all fine needle-point laces, and the returns of her trade in them, particularly with the court of France, the centre for such elegancies, are enormous. At this juncture the young king, taking counsel with his far-seeing minister Colbert, cast away the vexatious measures inspired a short time earlier by his mother, and forthwith determined to enrich his own kingdom with the means of pursuing an industry which had proved so remunerative to Venice. As lace-making was already to some extent practised in many parts of France, Alençon already enjoying a reputation for its skill in this direction, Colbert, with statesmanlike perception, set inquiries on foot respecting those towns whose local circumstances would best favour the contemplated development ; and selected them as special centres for the privileged manufacture of lace.

Monseigneur de Bonzy, bishop of Beziers, was then French Ambassador at Venice ; to him Colbert natur-

teenth centuries was one of the principal Adriatic ports belonging to the Venetian Republic. The peasants of the Ionian Islands and neighbouring Greek coast were noted for geometric-patterned drawn thread and cutwork, and many wares of such character must have been imported by the Venetians through Ragusa. Hence they appear to have been named *Points de Raguse*. Venice, with her unlimited artistic resources in the sixteenth century, developed richer versions of these laces, and her later seventeenth-century sumptuous foliated scroll patterns (hardly displaying Oriental feeling) completely superseded, at the time of the *Revolte des Passements*, the Greek laces or *Points de Raguse*. The poetical lament of the coterie at the hotel de Rambouillet, over the extinction of the *Points de Raguse*, is, I think, to be accepted as reflecting the condition above indicated, and, if so, furnishes but slender grounds for the supposition that the *Points de Raguse* entered into rivalry with the finer developments of Venetian lace, by which they were certainly superseded.

ally turned, and received from him many communications on the subject. "All the convents,"* writes Monseigneur de Bonzy, "and poor families make a living out of this lace-making." In another letter he says, "I see how easy it would be for you to establish the making of Venetian needlepoint laces in France, if you were to send over here a few of the best French lace-makers' daughters to be taught, so that in time they should impart their instruction to others in France." This suggestion was accepted. And a few years later (January 1673), M. le Comte d'Avaux having succeeded M. de Bonzy as ambassador at Venice, Colbert writes: "I have gladly received the collar of needlepoint lace worked in relief that you have sent me, and I find it very beautiful. I shall have it compared with those now being made by our own lace-makers, although I may tell you before-hand that as good specimens are now made in this kingdom" (fig. 96).

But it is worth while to follow all the steps taken by Colbert to establish lace-making in France which are described in the careful history of *Point d'Alençon*† compiled by Madame Despierres.

An exclusive privilege, dated August 5th, 1665, for ten years, together with a subsidy of 36,000 livres (about £2,700) was granted by the minister to a company, the first shareholders in which were Pluymers, Talon, and another Talon, surnamed de Beaufort, etc. The principal office and shop were opened at Paris in the hotel de Beaufort.

* The convent of San Zaccaria was the most noted for its fine needlepoint laces.

Histoire du Point d'Alençon, by Madame Despierres, p. 18.

As we have already pointed out preference in starting centres for the manufacture was shown for those towns already engaged in lace-making, whether with the needle or with bobbins ; the company thus expecting to find, ready to hand for its operations, such conditions as would best favour the attainment of the object in view. The principal centres were Aurillac, Sedan, Reims, le Quesnoy, Alençon, Arras, Loudun, etc.

The title of *Points de France* was given to all the laces made at these centres, without distinction as to variety in make. In order to adopt all the processes of foreign lace-making, the company engaged, at the king's cost, workers from Italy and Flanders, placing them at the different suitable centres. Voltaire says that thirty came from Venice and two hundred from Flanders.

The most brilliant results came from the Alençon centre, which accordingly stood first on the list. It is true that since the commencement of the seventeenth century Alençon had turned out needlepoint lace, and that some of the lace-makers there showed great talent in the art, and earned high wages. Marriage contracts and wills, the terms of which have been extracted by Madame Despierres, with the utmost care, furnish significant figures. A notable instance is that of a family named Barbot, the mother having amassed 500 livres (about £37 10s.). Her daughter, Marthe Barbot, married Michel. Mercier, sieur de la Perrière, on 18th March, 1633, and brought him a wedding portion of 300 livres (about £22 10s.), the earnings of her industry ; whilst her sister Suzanne Barbot's wedding portion upon her marriage with Paul Fenouillet, on 28th August, 1661, amounted to " 6,000 livres (about £450), earned in making cutworks and works *en vélin* (needlepoint lace done on a parchment pattern), which command a high price." This last sentence indicates that the elder sister, Madame de la Perrière, many years before the founding of the royal manufacture, had acquainted herself with the Venetian methods of making needlepoint laces.

It seems quite evident here, that the difference between the point lace made at Alençon before 1665, and that made by Madame de la Perrière, on her own initiative, in imitation of Venetian specimens for which Colbert established a special manufacture, was one in respect of design or pattern, and quality of work. Point on vellum (*point en vélin*), so termed because the work was done on a vellum or parchment pattern, had been wrought at Alençon for fifty years. It was evidently the same as that, rightly called by the Italians *punto in aere*, made on parchment patterns, but usually of geometric character ; survivals, indeed, of kindred patterns for cutworks and cognate open embroideries, which by the circulation of pattern books for a hundred and fifty years, *i.e.*, from 1500 to 1650, had become generally known throughout Europe.

But what had meanwhile given new features to Venetian laces was a departure, reflecting the greatest taste in the composition of patterns, and consisting of flowering and interlacing scrolls, blossomed with flowers "worked over in relief," as Colbert says in his letter to Comte d'Avaux, and enriched with most admirable details.

From the lace insertions and dentated borders of the sixteenth century, to the laces of flowering scrolls brought to high perfection by the Venetians in 1640, a considerable progress had taken place which Louis XIV. and Colbert fully appreciated. And it was in the direction of extending this progress that the Grande Monarque and his minister introduced subtle developments at Alençon and other centres of the royal manufacture.

Surrounded as he was by artists who furnished designs for all works undertaken for his court, Louis XIV. would not have contented himself for long with simple copies of the patterns brought over by the Venetian lace-workers who had been engaged to teach their art in France. The studios of the Gobelins, where a bevy of talented designers for tapestries, costumes, and festive decorations was regularly employed, must certainly have supplied designs for the lace manufactures.* Who indeed can now say whether the transformation in the patterns of Venetian laces, of which but little trace is to be detected in the Italian pattern books, was not largely owing to the orders sent from the French court ?

During that time the Venetian Senate, exercising a vigilant guardianship over the interests of the Republic, regarded the departure of Venetian workers to France as a State crime. Forthwith was issued the following decree, the severity of which is out of tune with modern ideas :—

" If any artist or handicraftsman practises his art in any foreign land, to the detriment of the Republic,

* In the accounts of the king's buildings is the entry of a payment to " Bailly, the painter, for several days' work with other painters, in making designs for embroideries and *Points d'Espagne.*"

orders to return will be sent to him ; if he disobeys them his nearest of kin will be put into prison in order that through his interest in their welfare his obedience may be compelled. If he comes back, his past offence will be condoned, and employment for him will be found in Venice ; but if, notwithstanding the imprisonment of his nearest of kin, he obstinately decides to continue living abroad, an emissary will be commissioned to kill him, and his next of kin will only be liberated upon his death."*

This decree applied not only to the lace-makers but also to the glass and mirror-makers whom Louis XIV. had induced to come to France.

Happily no emissaries were deputed to carry into effect the terrible threats held over these truant workpeople. The experiment of bringing Venetian lace-workers to France required no repetition ; the women were free to return with sufficient promptitude to their native land, since the first attempt had answered admirably ; for, as Voltaire writes, in a short space of time sixteen hundred girls were in full occupation at lace-making at the royal centres of the industry.

The production of the *Points de Venise*, and consequently of the *Points de France* which in many cases involved the closest imitation of the Venetian stitches, was all that could be wished. As rapidly as patterns became elaborated from the times of Louis XIII., so quality in the craft of reproducing them as laces improved. A close and detailed inspection of the splendid rabato or neck-band in the Cluny Museum (No. 6,587 in the Catalogue) is indispensable to any

* *Venice*, by Charles Yriarte, p. 228.

one who wants to really appreciate the extraordinary standard of work to which the art of the needle can attain (fig. 96). Nothing in embroidery can compare with such marvels of elegance, delicacy, and at the same time vigour, as those displayed in this specimen

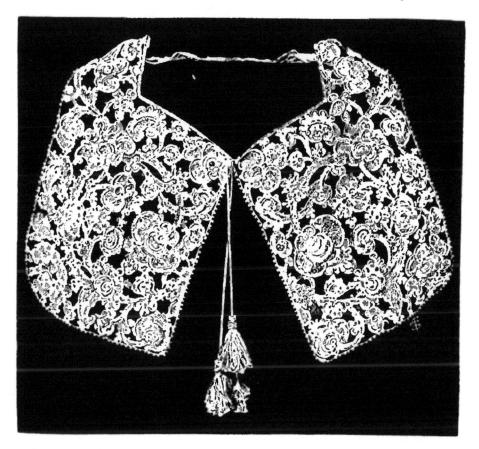

Fig. 96.—Splendid rabato of Venetian needlepoint lace (in the Cluny Museum).

of needlepoint lace. Not only do the scrolls of the design flow with dignity and grace, but the lace-worker herself would appear to have invented an almost super-abundance of wonderfully dainty devices, giving light-ness in effect to the otherwise heavy forms of the flowers. Firmness of outline marking the different

contours, results from employing a horsehair, over which
minute stitches are cast; and by the same means a

Fig. 97.—Venetian needlepoint lace (seventeenth century).

finished crispness is imparted to tiny loops or *picots*
elegantly inserted in the spaces between the scrolls and
flowers. This method is still in use in the making of

Points d'Alençon which for sharp definition bear the palm over other laces. It is related of a collar made at Venice for Louis XIV., that the lace-workers being unsuccessful in finding sufficiently fine horsehair employed some of their own hairs instead, in order to secure that marvellous delicacy of work which they aimed at producing. The specimen cost 250 golden *écus* (about £60).

It was for men, then, that these magnificent things were made. They were chiefly in the form of rabatos* or bands falling from beneath the chin over the breast, the fashion for which, succeeding that of ruffs and collars, when large wigs were worn (fig. 98). Cuffs of similar fine lace were also worn. These latter were occasionally so large that Molière was incited to write

De ces manches, qu'à table on voit tâter les sauces.†

Fine *guipure* laces of this character are also to be seen in rochets worn by Bossuet (fig. 99), Fenelon, and other prelates, whose portraits are well worth referring to according to the indications of them given by G. Duplessis.

Ladies trimmed their *berthes* and sleeves with these *guipures*; when the sleeves were short they were called *engageantes*; when long, *pagodes*. Upon skirts laces were worn, *volantes* or as flounces, whence the name *volant* or flounce, which has come into use for all

* Towards the end of Louis XIV.'s reign flat rabatos were superseded by others which fell in folds, and were called *cravates*, after, it is said the Croates, or Croatian guards who were much esteemed by Maria Theresa of Austria.

† *École des Maris.*

wide laces; these flouncings were draped either in *tournantes* or *quilles*; the former laid horizontally, the latter vertically upon skirts; but in either case these were stitched down on each edge of the

Fig. 98 —Louis XIV., 1670 (after Hyacinthe Rigaud).

lace, whereas flounces were fastened to dresses by the *engrelure* or footing, a small band along the upper border of a flounce. Lace *barbes* and *fontages* (a sort of erection like a sheaf of lace) were used as head-dresses ; besides these, handkerchiefs, *fichus*, scarves, mantillas thrown over the head, and mantles across the shoulders, were all trimmed with lace.

Berain and Le Brun gave a new and most artistic turn to patterns for laces, which fully justified the success achieved. In portraits painted immediately after 1665, the year when the Royal Alençon manufacture was started, we have sufficient data for recognizing the style of the first *points de France* designed by the king's artists. The laces, to be there noted, are entirely of a French character with ornamental *motifs* more or less emblematical of the attributes belonging to the Sun King.

Fig. 99.—Fragment of an alb or rochet of *Point de France* (from an engraving by Drevet of Bcssuet's portrait).

It may be gathered, from what we have said, that towards the end of the seventeenth century the make of French laces was identical with that of the Venetian, the difference between the two classes being one solely in respect of pattern. At Venice patterns retained their Italian character of graceful scrolls embellished with rich floral and blossom devices, of an Oriental flavour perhaps, suggestive in a measure of those dreams without termination

or definite climax which are so entirely in the vein of
Arabian or Persian poetry.

In French contemporary lace patterns we observe
a tendency to similar ornament, which, however, is
treated in a more precise and less dreamy manner,
and intermixed with ideal architectural elements of
an extremely light character, generally subordinated to
well-balanced arrangement of grouping about some
central device possessing strongly marked symbolism.

This style of pattern, based upon a regularity in
arrangement of its component parts, gave birth to an
influence the effects of which seem to be visible in
some of the smallest of the details in the lace ornamentation at this period. We have no hesitation in
attributing to this influence, for regularity in arrangement, the germs of that important transition to grounds
of regular meshes. Little by little the intercrossing
and arbitrarily placed bars or *brides* which contrasted
pleasantly with the devices in the composition of a
pattern, were subjected to a regularity in arrangement.

The fine flounce of *Point de France* (fig. 100) filled
with personages, portraits, and emblems of the time
of Louis XIV., is an illustration of the transition to
regular grounds just mentioned. The specimen has
for many years been in the possession of Madame
Dupré of Tours; and Léon Palustre assigns a date
between 1675 and 1680 for its production. The
ground consists of bars with tiny loops on each,
(*brides à picots*) similar in workmanship to Venetian
brides, but arranged in a series of hexagonal shapes
thus forming a ground of regular large meshes, the

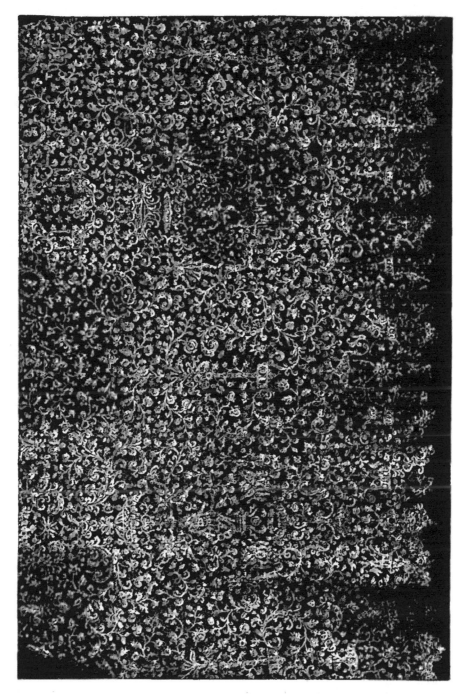

Fig. 100.—Flounce of *Point de France*, in the pattern of which are introduced figures and attributes of Louis XIV.'s reign.

orderly arrangement of which corresponds with that

regulating the disposition of the larger devices in the pattern.

At this time *Point de France* is supreme. Watteau's painting of the Presentation of the Grand Dauphin in 1668 displays the babe robed in "Holland linen enriched with *Points de France*." When the Prince de Conti marries Mademoiselle de Blois, the king's wedding gift is a set of toilet hangings, all trimmed with *Points de France.*" It is of Mademoiselle de Blois that Madame de Sévigné writes in a letter dated 27th January, 1674, describing her as "beautiful as an angel with a *tablier* and *bavette* of *Point de France*" (a sort of panel on the front of the body to her dress, and a large one on the front of the skirt).

Before discussing the different classes of laces with meshed grounds (*à réseaux*) we must say a few words about the term which really applies to the larger section of older laces, that is *guipure.*

Originally the term was used in connection with cord composed of an inner core or stout thread, whipped round with fine threads, and the name in this sense is used by trimming and gimp-makers of the present day. With cords of gimp of this description (*cordonnet-guipure*) trimming ornaments were made, which were frequently stitched (*appliqués*), on to a stuff, after the manner of the furniture hangings belonging to Catherine de Médicis, which are described as "velvet hangings with white gimp (*guipure*) ornaments, besides cloths of gold and of silver and dove-colour, with figures and scrolls of gold gimp and tinsel.*

Lace-makers also employed gimp for bars and tyes in

* Inventory already quoted by Bonnaffé (see p. 131).

imitation of the dainty *brides à picots* of the Venetians. This, by degrees, gave rise to an extension in the use of the term *guipure*, and its subsequent application to all laces in which bars or tyes were used; whilst those, in which the grounds were of small regular meshes (*réseaux*), were distinguished under the name *dentelles*. Hence it may be right to speak of all those splendid laces with their bars (*brides*) embellished with tiny loops (*picots*), little stars, and semilunes, the fame of which reflected glory* upon the city of the Doges, as "*Guipures de Venise*."

To recapitulate briefly, the reign of Louis XIV. is notable for the display both of the Venetian *guipures* in their most sumptuous development, and of *Points de France*, which touched the highest standard of magnificence possible in needlepoint laces. But variations in pattern and make, broadly classifiable under these two groups, are not so numerous as those which arose in the succeeding reign of wild caprices in taste The pre-eminently artistic character of lace made during Louis XIV.'s period has, however, never been surpassed.

---

* Amongst portraits at Venice, ornamented with the finest *guipures*, we may cite that of the Dogeress Quirini Vallier and that of Morosina Morosini, wife of Doge Marino Grimani.

CHAPTER III.

In the sixteenth and seventeenth centuries the grounds of laces may be broadly described to have been varied and irregular, like those in *guipures*. Meshed grounds (*réseaux*) when they first appeared were subordinate accessories to a pattern. In the eighteenth century they play another part altogether; and we find them as grounds superseding the irregular barrings of the *guipures*.

The word *réseau*, formerly termed *réseuil*, is derived from *rets* (nets); and, as we have seen, *réseuil* was used as a descriptive name for the net ground of *lacis*. When laces with grounds of regular meshes came into fashion, *réseau* was the generic appellation for such grounds; and the varieties of special local makes of *réseaux* were known under the names of the several localities, whence we have the *réseau d'Alençon*, that of Argentan, and of Chantilly, Brussels, Mechlin and Valenciennes, etc.

Points de France, under Louis XIV., had more or less been distinguished by grounds of regular meshes, large in size and enriched with tiny loops or *picots*. The large mesh was, however, soon reduced to smaller dimensions, and thus the *petit réseau* (ground of small meshes) was evolved, in which the elegancies of little *picots*, etc., could not be used to break the monotony of regular meshes. Nevertheless, *réseaux* possess a peculiar charm, as we shall see in the case of the Argentan laces, where *réseaux* with meshes of various sizes have been happily contrasted in making up a ground. But their encroaching predominance in laces is coeval with a falling off in general artistic quality of design.

Of the *Points de France* at the commencement of the eighteenth century there is one variety—the *Point de Sedan*—which calls for some notice. Sedan was one of the lace centres selected by Colbert,[*] and to it no doubt belongs the greater share of the reputation attaching to this lace, which, however, was also made at Alençon; for the characteristics of *Points de Sedan* were merely such as resulted from a slightly varied arrangement of stitches, all of which were also worked at Alençon. The floral devices in *Points de Sedan*, somewhat large, and heavy in execution, spring from bold scroll forms, and in between them are big meshes of the *grande maille picotée*, of the *Point de France*. Instead of an even and slightly raised stitching along their contours, these big flowers are accentuated here and there in well-chosen parts by raised stitching, worked somewhat with the effect of vigorous touches of rather forced high lights in a picture. These recurrent little mounds of relief, as they may be called, are frequently introduced with admirable artistic result. The finest bishops' rochets, which appear in the later portraits by Hyacinthe Rigaud and De Largillière, are of *Point de Sedan*. But this lace soon became tainted

* See Louis XIV.'s letter of the 9th November, 1666, addressed to M. de la Bourlie, Governor of Sedan.

with the pretentiousness of the rococo style so much
affected during the Regency, and one can express but
a guarded admiration of works bearing the impress of
this style.

Alençon made a speciality of very regular mesh
grounds. At first the meshes were large, similar to the
hexagonal barring (*brides*) of the *Point de France*, but
quite simple and without *picots* (fig. 101); refinements in
making the ground ensued, and the button-hole stitched
barring was gradually felt to be too clumsy for delicate
work; accordingly a lighter and more simply constructed
mesh was invented, and this has survived as the perfected hexagonal mesh known in all countries as
distinctive of the Alençon ground or *réseau*.

During the transition in the make of meshes, Argentan
simplified the method of producing the larger hexagonal
meshes. As has been said, they were first constructed
by means of button-hole stitching, but instead of this the
Argentan workers took to a *bride tortillée;* that is, twisting
or whipping thread around each of the six *brides* which
form a single mesh. To fix the twisted thread on each
bride, a button-hole stitch was taken on commencing the
twisting, and a second one on its termination at the
other end of the *bride*. This simplification in producing
a *bride* mesh is well explained by Madame Despierres
in her history of Alençon laces. The facility with
which this twisted *bride* mesh could be made, con-
duced to simpler and more economical work, the
results of which obtained considerable vogue in the
middle of the eighteenth century, and were generally
known (especially in laces with large meshes made in
this way) as *Points d'Argentan*. Laces in which these

Argentan bride meshes are happily blended or contrasted with smaller mesh grounds (of the *Point*

Fig. 101.—Point d'Alençon with hexagonal *bride* ground or *réseau*, commencement of the eighteenth century.

d'Alençon class) are frequently of the choicest description.

But the grounds of regular meshes led to an impover-
ishment in the patterns of laces, and when this was
perceived, ingenuity devised the employment of little
fanciful devices (*jours* or *modes*) with which the centres
of blossoms and other appropriate spaces in the pattern
would be filled in.   From these *modes* or fillings sprang
a series of most charming little devices, in which the
skilfully plied needle often surpassed all that it had
previously effected.   Such fillings or *modes* will be
found generally to be inserted like little jewellings in
the centres of blossom forms, though they also spread
over wider spaces, as in medallions, shells, or spaces
between garlands and along the borders of laces.   Some
of these fillings (*jours* or *modes*) were even used as
entire grounds for such laces as were to be richer in
effect than when made with simple mesh grounds.
And one of these fillings used as a ground, greatly
favoured at the beginning of the eighteenth century,
has been named by Mrs. Bury-Palliser Argentella
ground—a name which has given rise to discussion.*

The great success of the Alençon and Argentan
centres of the lace industry raised up many competitors
with them.

In the first place, Venice, finding that laces of lighter
texture were being sought after, that men wore less as
women wore more of them, introduced refinements in her
productions, and, in lieu of the vigorous scrolls with
rich reliefs, such as she had made in the seventeenth
century, she set herself to make the *point de rose* (rose-

---

* Alan S. Cole, *Les Dentelles Anciennes*, translated by C. P. Haus-
soullier. (The English edition is *Ancient Needlepoint and Pillow Lace*.
Arundel Society.   1874.)

point) and other laces, the patterns in which resemble coral branches. Rosepoint is a Venetian needlepoint

Fig. 102.—Venetian needlepoint lace (rosepoint), eighteenth century (belonging to Madame G. Dreyfus).

lace of delicate scrolls enriched with many little off-shoots, held together by tiny bars or *brides à picots*, and freely spotted with small blossoms consisting of wreaths of microscopic loops or *picots* superposed one on the other with the daintiest effect (fig. 102). This lace, infinitely less bold than the great and splendid Venetian *guipures*, is more elegant and precious looking, and reflects eighteenth-century taste for pettiness of detail.

According to Zeno of Udine, Joseph II., Emperor of Germany (1765—1790), ordered on the occasion of his marriage a set of rosepoint laces at a cost of thirty thousand florins, which from all accounts seem to have been of the finest quality ever reached in this style.

Attempts were also made at Venice to produce needlepoint laces with meshed grounds. Burano, one of the islands in the lagoon, gave its name to a lace with a ground of meshes; but no slightly raised overcast outlines (*festons*) were used to mark its details, as is the case with *Point d'Alençon*, and with later Burano lace, such as that shown in fig. 112. The outline of the ornaments in Burano lace, and indeed in all the late seventeenth and early eighteenth century Venetian laces made with meshed grounds, are of scarcely perceptible single threads. It seems as though the Venetians did not grasp the extent of variations in effect of which filmy needlepoint laces are capable.*

* I may here note that M. Lefébure refrains from mentioning a class of fine needlepoint lace which has been termed by many (Monsieur Dupont-Auberville amongst them) *Point de Venise à réseau*. For employment of wonderfully fine thread this class of lace is remarkable. But there is a formality in its patterns which appears to have succumbed before, and been altogether superseded by, the floral playfulness of the French and Flemish contemporary laces. Hence *Point de Venise à réseau* is rare. Fig. 103, although called by Monsieur

Flanders, which hitherto had almost entirely restricted her making of laces to the pillow or bobbin method, soon attempted to copy the needlepoint laces of Alençon. The needlepoint laces made at Brussels were flatter and less firm than the *Points d'Alençon*, and in some instances were of finer texture (fig. 103). Belgium spun the most slender and delicate of all flax threads: Felix Aubry states that it was sold at

Fig. 103.—Flemish needlepoint lace, end of the seventeenth century (belonging to Madame Franck).

from eight to ten thousand francs (£320 to £400) the pound weight. Hence it will be understood that with such dainty material laces of the utmost filminess could be produced; and the variety of little open devices (*jours* or *modes*) was multiplied with charming

Lefébure Flemish needlepoint lace of the late seventeenth century, might, I think, be equally entitled to the name *Point de Venise à réseau*. Certain differences between Flemish needlepoint lace (the *Point à l'aiguille de Bruxelles*) and the *Point de Venise à réseau* are stated in *Ancient Needlepoint and Pillow Lace*.

dexterity, and ranked amongst the triumphs of Brussels needlepoint.

As fashion favoured the application (*appliqué*) of floral devices, made in pillow lace, to meshed grounds separately made (as we shall explain later), laces known as *Points d'Angleterre*, had a great success. One of the kinds of application lace consisted of floral devices, etc., made in needlepoint, and applied or stitched on to pillow-made mesh grounds (*vrai réseau de Bruxelles*). Some of the more sumptuous of the *Points d'Angleterre* are made in this manner. The exquisite softness of the meshed ground, the dainty workmanship in the flowers, of which the outlines (*cordonnets*) have little or no relief, the gem-like wealth of the fillings (*jours* or *modes*), have placed these Brussels points in a category quite distinct from those of Alençon, Argentan, and Venice, which are more remarkable for their firmness of texture and crisp accentuation of their reliefs.

Supple light and beautiful lappets for the head were made in Brussels point, and during certain phases of fashion were preferred before similar but rather heavier things made in *Point de France* or *Point d'Alençon*. Although etiquette required that at court presentations ladies should wear only point lace lappets on their heads, the Brussels points were deemed to comply with this regulation.

These court presentations were attended with much ceremony and show. When a lady had secured the privilege of such honour, she arrived at the appointed hour and presented herself at the door of the grand chamber, waiting her turn to be called in, dressed in the most magnificent stuffs, tricked out with the finest point laces of her wardrobe, and glittering with all the diamonds she could collect from the jewel-boxes of her relations. A court robe or train trailing behind her eight ells in length was fastened to her waist, and from her hair, cunningly plumed, hung point lace lappets, falling in the regulation lengths prescribed for respective degrees of nobility. Every detail of this sort was subject to minute rule. Princesses of the blood alone enjoyed the right of wearing full length lappets in their head-dresses.

The use of finery, thus encouraged under Louis XIV. in reception-rooms, was in Louis XV.'s reign extended to boudoirs and bedrooms. Never were dishabilles more elegant; coverlets of beds, trimmings of curtains and pillow-cases, of toilet tables, etc., involved a consumption of laces far in excess of what had been necessary for dresses in the preceding reign.

The Marquise de Créquy, speaking of her aunt, the Dowager Duchesse de la Ferté, said that she had, in 1714, a quilt made of one single piece of Venetian point. "I am certain," she adds, "that the trimmings of her curtains, which were of *Point d'Argentan*, were worth at least forty thousand écus."

At this date two rival manufacturers at Argentan contended for workpeople,* and their disputes indicate how much store was set upon *Point d'Argentan*. One of them, named Duponchel, complained that Mdlle. James, his competitor, enticed his workwomen from him, and sought special protection on the grounds that

* Madame Despierres, *Histoire du Point d'Alençon*, p. 95.

he worked for the king and his court. On the other hand, Mdlle. James maintained to the king's steward

Fig. 104.—Fragment of Point d'Alençon lace, early period of Louis XVI.

that "it is I who supplied laces for the king's chamber this year, by order of the Duc de Richelieu. I also have the honour of furnishing the king's wardrobe, by order of the Duc de la Rochefoucauld. Moreover, I am purveyor to the King and Queen of Spain, and at this very moment I am engaged in supplying lace for the marriage of the Dauphin " (Letter of the 9th September, 1744). Duponchel rejoins that " he had supplied two *toilettes* and their *suites*, several *bourgognes* (ladies' head-dresses), as well as a cravat for the queen."

The number of lace-makers then at work was at least 1,200 at Argentan and its vicinity ; whilst at Alençon and the neighbouring villages it is said that there were 8,000. Boucher, the painter, appears to have preferred *Point d'Argentan* ; and no one knew better than he how to make charming effects in his patterns, by contrasting and interchanging the delicate and bolder grounds which are so characteristic of this lace.

Under Louis XVI. the taste for great lightness in design proved unfavourable to needlepoint laces. Instead of point laces, worn flatly for the display of all the daintinesses of their exquisite fillings and delicate reliefs, it became the fashion to multiply the number of flounces to dresses and to gather them into small pleats, or, as it was termed, *badiner* them, so that the ornamental motives, more or less broken up or partially concealed by the pleats, lost their decorative value. The spaces between the motives were therefore widened more and more, until at last nothing was left but grounds of meshes, very slightly ornamented with flowers ; or else these grounds would be powdered over (*semés*) with tiny blossoms and sprays—a style of design which offered little opportunity for invention, especially when the little devices to be used were restricted to peas or dots.

The kinds of laces with powderings of such insignificant ornaments, and suitable for gathering into pleats or being fluted, were more successfully produced on the pillow, and were altogether of a more filmy nature than the needlepoint laces. Nevertheless a considerable quantity was made of similarly patterned *Points d'Alençon à petites brides.** This ground of *petites brides* consists of meshes made with twisted threads in the manner of that of the *Point d'Argentan*, as described on page 228, but more closely twisted. The effect is rather cloudy and thick. The greater number of men's *jabots* (shirt frills or neckerchiefs), which, in Louis XVI.'s reign, fell in pleats over the openings of their long waistcoats, were usually of *Point d'Alençon à petite bride* (fig. 105). This kind of lace is very compact in make, and stands much washing, which at that time was rendered necessary through the fashionable habit of snuffing, the yellow stains from which often displayed themselves upon the frills of noble counts and marquises.

The Revolution contributed to ruin the manufacture of needlepoint laces. Many districts were severely tried, and the traditions of an art, which had been their former glory and profit, were lost. For close upon fifty years, Argentan and Venice herself—illustrious Venice—produced no more laces.

Alençon fared better. Napoleon, solicitous for a

---

* Madame Vigée-Lebrun, in one of her prettiest portraits, wears a *Point d Alençon* powdered lace (*à petits semés*).

revival of the manufacture, encouraged it, and endeavoured to renew the courtly etiquette of Louis XIV.
in requiring point lace to be worn at court receptions.
Some few important orders were given by the imperial
circle, and a bed-trimming of lace, powdered over with
bee devices, and costing 40,000 francs, is cited as an
instance. It is true that it was begun for the Empress
Josephine, and that in the course of its making her
escutcheons were replaced by those of Marie-Louise !

Fig. 105.—Point d'Alençon, with ground of small hexagonal *meshes*
(*à petite bride*), later period of Louis XVI.

who, little flattered by the notion of possessing what
had been destined for another, made difficulties about
receiving it.

In May 1811 the Emperor and Empress visited
Alençon. Marie-Louise received the lace-makers at
the Prefecture, saw them at work, and made a number
of purchases. Napoleon remarked, "It is marvellous
how well they work in France ! I ought to encourage
such an industry." But incessant wars frustrated any

Fig. 106.—Flounce of Point d'Alençon of modern manufacture.

real extension of trade in luxuries like lace, and constantly, interrupted commercial relations with foreign countries. Russia before others has always shown a liking for *Point d'Alençon.*

Peace restored prosperity to Alençon ; and at each of the great international exhibitions she has secured the highest prizes for her sumptuous works of the needle (fig. 106). Hers are still the more dexterously

Fig. 107.—Belgian needlepoint lace, modern manufacture.

wrought and costly of laces, and she proves herself worthy of her illustrious past.

Latterly, Argentan has once more renewed the practice of her almost forgotten art, and the traditions have been revived of her laces with large meshes enhanced by fillings of small mesh grounds (*réseaux*) (fig. 108).

16

Bayeux has witnessed the establishment of a model

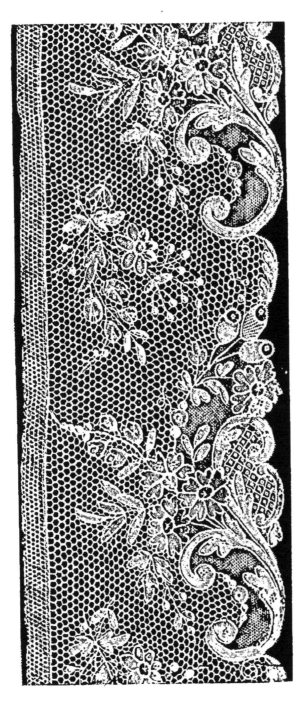

Fig. 108.—Point d'Argentan, modern manufacture.

workshop for needlepoint laces, where the making of many varieties of point lace is revived which, if not forgotten, had certainly been abandoned since the Revolution. Every sort of needlepoint lace made during the best periods can be produced now. The name *Point Colbert*, adopted in grateful memory of the great minister, protector of lace, is applied to point laces in high relief, with scrolls enriched with magnificent blossoms and flowers, with grounds of bars ornamented with dainty *picots* (loops), in pre-

cisely the same fashion as that of those laces made
by the Venetian mistresses of their craft who were
brought to Alençon in 1665 (see figs. 109 and 111).

Belgium has not been behindhand in the matter of
needlepoint lace-making : if *Point d'Alençon* remains,
according to hallowed expression, the Queen of Laces,

Fig. 109.—Collar of needlepoint lace (modern) worked at Bayeux,
and called Point Colbert.

Brussels and its neighbourhood produce a vast quantity
of ably wrought needlepoint laces, under the name of
"*Point Gaze*" (fig. 107). The shawl (fig. 110) is a
beautiful specimen of such work. The *feston* or outline
to the ornament in *Point Gaze* has no horsehair in
it, and is not therefore so firm and crisp in appearance as that of *Point d'Alençon*. But the fillings
(*jours*) are of cunning work and great diversity. The

floral ornaments are cleverly depicted with delicate gradations of close and open textures. The export of this lace, to America particularly, is very considerable at times. Unfortunately the manufacture of flax threads as fine as those of earlier dates is almost

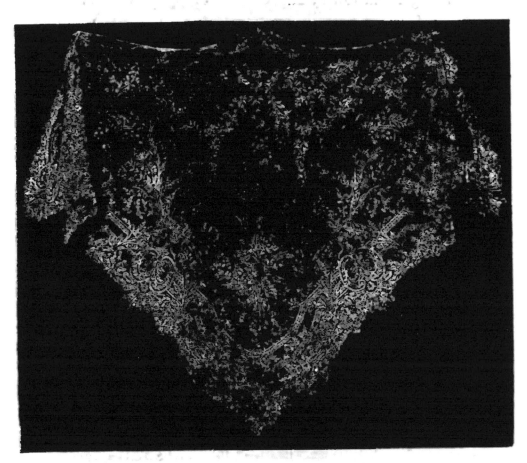

Fig. 110.—Shawl of Belgian needlepoint lace (modern), from a design by Alcide Roussel.

extinct; and many of the modern laces are made with cotton instead of flax. Nevertheless, whatever orders she is called upon to meet, Belgium carries them out with skill untrammelled by routine (fig. 113). In questions of pattern the impulse of novelty and style comes from Paris, which fairly claims to be the

Fig. 111.—Cuff of needlepoint lace (modern) called Point Colbert.

foremost inspirer of artistic motive in all lace production.

Fig. 112.—Point de Burano, of modern Belgian
manufacture.

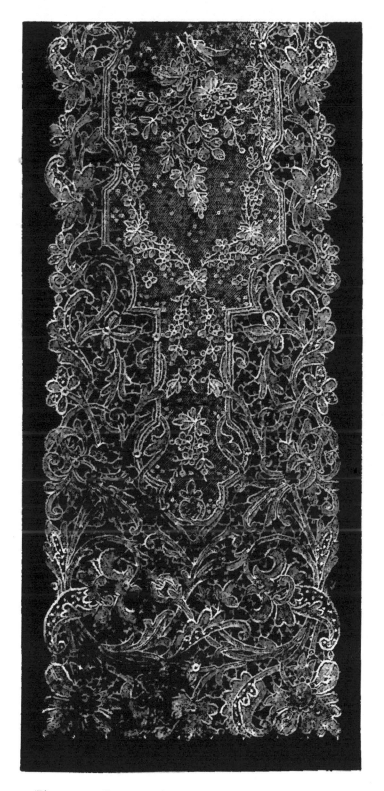

Fig. 113.—Lappet of modern needlepoint lace.

Obedient to the dictates of that invisible but supreme queen, named fashion, the making of these different laces in France, as in Belgium, is more or less extensive, and prospers.

High patronage within recent years has revived Venetian lace-making, which had died out. Under its auspices a school of lace-workers has been established in the island of Burano, a name already mentioned.

Fig. 114.—Irish crochet lace (*Point d'Irlande*).

"The little isle of Burano," writes an Italian author, "is situated two leagues to the north-east of Venice; it is the poorest of the archipelago in the lagoon, and withal the richest in beautiful and steady young girls." Lace-making, as one sees, retains its former place as the occupation of the *virtuose donne*. Some admirable copies of ancient laces made at the Burano school were exhibited in Paris at the Exhibition in 1878.

Austria's contribution to this Exhibition, and that of

Vienna in 1882, consisted of needlepoint laces, for the most part copies of old specimens in her Museum of Industrial Art. In Austria and Hungary there are

Fig. 115.—Flounce of Limerick lace (Ireland), embroidery on net.

many able hands, requiring but well-regulated encouragement to evoke a more serious development of their industry.

At Moscow, in Russia, a lace school produces capital

work, bearing the impress of a Russian taste which leans to a Byzantine style of art.

Lastly, we may mention Ireland, where for some

Fig. 116.—Part of a flounce of Kenmare lace (Ireland), flat and slightly raised needlepoint lace.

time lace-making has been pursued. At the time of the famine in 1846 special efforts were made to encourage the industry as a means of assisting a suffering, poverty-stricken population in the "Emerald Isle." The story goes that the first piece of Venetian lace used as a pattern in Ireland was procured by a Jesuit, and much of the needlepoint lace has been since called "Jesuit lace." In the schools attached to many convents the girls are trained to embroider on net, and to do needlepoint lace. Crochet lace-

Fig. 117.—Borders of New Ross lace (Ireland), raised needlepoint lace.

making is a speciality (see fig. 114), from which much better results could be obtained. The Department of Science and Art of the Committee of Council on Education has latterly been called upon to aid in the development of the Irish lace industry.*

* The particular form of encouragement given by this Department has been that of payments on results of instruction in drawing and

In crochet lace, which starts from no foundation, as does embroidery with a crochet needle (see p. 4), the work is done upon no tracing on parchment or paper : the work is done in the hand, very much after the manner of knitting. The thread is looped, pulled through the loop as in chain-stitch, knotted, and so forth. By a series of interlocking chain-stitches this crochet lace is produced. Without attaining to great

Fig. 118.—Border of Youghal lace (Ireland), flat needlepoint lace.

value, this class of work is capable of considerable refinement.

Summary.—This slight sketch of needle-made laces

design. Within the last few years lace-making convents have established drawing and designing classes in connection with their lace-schools. These drawing classes are branches of schools of art at Cork and Waterford. The Cork School of Art, under the able guidance of Mr. James Brenan, R.H.A., now supplies lace-schools with patterns for the various classes of Irish lacework. Fig. 115 displays a flounce of embroidery on net worked at Limerick from a design by a student of the school ; fig. 116 is part of a flounce worked at the convent of Poor Clares Kenmare, in needlepoint lace, from a design by Miss Julyan, of the Dublin Metropolitan School of Art ;

will at least show what an important part they have played in sumptuary arts from the fifteenth century to our days.

It is to be noted that these laces have almost in-

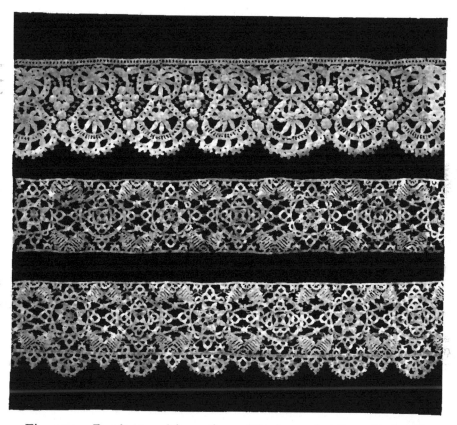

Fig. 119.—Borders and insertion of Cork crochet lace (Ireland).

variably been made of white thread. The needle seems to have disdained using any fantastic threads; and

fig. 117 shows two borders of raised needlepoint lace made at the Carmelite Convent, New Ross, from designs by the master of the Waterford School of Art; fig. 118 is a border of dainty needlepoint lace made at Youghal from a design by the mistress of the Dublin School of Art; and fig. 119 shows some crochet recently made at Cork from new designs by Mr. Holland. Carrickmacross lace consists of cut cambric *guipure* and cut cambric *appliqué* on net. Fig. 120 is of a border and insertion of the latter class of lacework from designs by Miss Anderson.

specimens in which coloured or gold and silver threads have been employed are excessively rare ; such materials have been more frequently used for pillow-made laces. The delicate sculpturesque creations of the needle, with gradations of gentle relief, may be said to be comparable with other laces, as marbles culpture is with wood-

Fig. 120.—Border and insertion of Carrickmacross lace (Ireland), *appliqué* and other embroidery on net.

carving. Charles Blanc, comparing the two classes of hand-made laces, makes the following very apposite remarks :—

" The dominant character of pillow-made laces is the soft blending of its forms : the needle is to the bobbin and pillow what the pencil point is to the stump. The pattern—of which the definition becomes softened when wrought in pillow lace—is depicted with crispness by the needle." This in a measure accounts for the relative importance of needlepoint lace, and its higher value. Point lace is most suited to occasions of state, and rightly possesses an universally recognized prestige.

Notwithstanding many severe trials and ups and downs, the traditions of this beautiful art are not lost. Modern eclecticism, perhaps, even engenders a number of favourable circumstances : it is possible nowadays to reproduce the finest works of other notable times, and there is no lack of skilful workers. Artists and people of taste know how to appreciate the refinements of old laces. If instead of incontinently decrying modern lace they would encourage the execution of well-considered commissions, there is little doubt that modern art could produce results as excellent as those of past centuries. May we then have inspired our readers with a lively interest for the noble and charming art of needlepoint lace-making, which fascinated Louis XIV. and Colbert, and by which many towns and villages have acquired legitimate renown !

BOBBIN OR PILLOW-MADE LACES.

CHAPTER I.

FROM THEIR ORIGIN TO THE END OF THE REIGN OF LOUIS XIV.

Manufacture.—We have already explained the make of bobbin or pillow laces; briefly, they are tissues produced by intercrossing and plaiting the threads, which are rolled at one end around bobbins and fastened at the other upon a cushion or pillow by means of pins.

Bobbins.—Bobbins (fig. 9) are called *fuseaux* or *bloquets* in French, and *fuselli* or *piombini* in Italian; the latter term apparently implies little shaped blocks of lead. Bobbins were also made of bone, whence the Italian name *ossi*, and the English, bones. But it is customary to speak of them in English as bobbins. They are, in fact, small elongated spindles or reels tapering and swelling at one end into little handles for convenience of manipulation.

The size of bobbins varies according to the usage of districts and the thickness of threads employed. In Belgium bobbins, generally thin and very light, are appropriate for the making of filmy fabrics like Valenciennes and Mechlin laces; in Auvergne, on the contrary, where stout *guipures* or *torchon* laces are made, involving the use of very different materials, bobbins are much larger. But pillow lace-makers frequently use, for the same piece of work, bobbins of different sizes, in order to readily distinguish the different degrees of thread corresponding with the different bobbins upon which they are respectively wound.

Sometimes a small covering of thin horn is placed around the head of the bobbin, to protect and keep clean from dust its supply of thread. In Normandy these little coverings are called *noquettes*.

Pillows or *Cushions*.—These are of greater variety even than the bobbins. Some are square, some cylindrical, some pyramidal, some like drums, and some like large pincushions with firm flat base. In England they are generally pillows or cushions (as in fig. 11), and when used without a stand are held on the lap ; in Italy they are called *tombola*.

Small and flattened cushions are used in Belgium for making single devices and flowers for *appliqué* lace ; long cushions are used at Barcelona ; big cushions (fig. 10), upon which upwards of six hundred bobbins may be used, are employed for making delicate laces, as at Bayeux. But the bulkiest forms of cushion are those of the *almofadas*, or species of drum, which the Portuguese of Vianna do Castello or of Peniche gracefully place between their feet on end upon a basket high enough to bring the cushion level with their hands.

Pricking the Patterns.—The pattern over which a pillow lace is made is traced and pricked upon a card or bit of parchment of close and smooth surface, so that the threads, as thrown one over the other,

17

may not be caught by any little irregularity. The pricked holes show the worker where she is to stick her pins as *points d'arrêt* for the formation of the several stitches. In certain classes of laces as many pin-holes or prickings are necessary as there are meshes in the network of the ground. By means of the prickings, as well as directions written across floral or other ornamental devices of the pattern, several lace-makers, working quite independently, finish similar portions of patterns with such uniformity that the parts can be easily united together to make up one large piece of lace.

If the pattern, instead of being for a particular shape, as for a collar, a head-dress, or a lappet, is for a continuous band of some sort, consisting of repeats of the same ornament, the cushion may be fitted with a rotating cylinder, round which a complete repeat is fastened. With such an appliance, revolving as the work proceeds, the worker has a continuous pattern to work from. The method of two sorts of revolving endless patterns is displayed in figs. 10 and 11. It is, however, attended with one draw-back, and that is, that, as the threads have to hang in one direction, the make of the lace must follow that direction. Upon a flat cushion the making may spread out in all directions. The lace-worker using a revolving pattern meets with difficulties in rendering certain fillings in flowers, etc., which run across, instead of with, the pattern; whilst the worker upon a flat cushion is not similarly inconvenienced.

On the other hand, the making of lace by the yard is not suited to flat cushions, since each time that a piece of lace is completed up to the end of the pattern all the pins have to be taken out, and the completed portion of the lace has to be moved up to the head of the pattern and fixed there before its continuation is possible. This, of course, involves loss of time.

However, each kind of cushion or pillow has its peculiar advantages and inconveniences. That best adapted to the special class of lace made in a district is naturally the one most commonly in use there.

Origin of Pillow Lace.—For a long time the question whether pillow-made lace was older in origin than needlepoint lace has been discussed. But it is unlikely that one should be earlier than the other, since the development and use of both sorts of lace are identified with the same period.

Flanders, conceding to Venice priority in needle-point lace-making, lays claim to the honour of having invented the bobbin or pillow method. Up to the present time no serious or definitive proof has been produced to substantiate this claim. J. Séguin offers the following reasons to show that Belgium did not make pillow lace sooner than Italy :—

The only pattern-books published in Belgium are those of Wilhem Vostermans, who died at Antwerp in 1542, and of Jean de Glen, who died at Liège in 1597. Neither contain patterns for bobbin or pillow laces.

No Flemish portrait earlier than the end of the sixteenth century shows laces upon costume, whereas after that time they abound plentifully.

The Church of St. Gomar, at Lierre, in the province

of Antwerp, possesses a *retable*, said to have been painted in 1495 by Quentin Matsys, in which, amongst other figures, is one of a young girl making lace on a pillow. But connoisseurs deny the authorship attributed to this painting, and consider the work to be by Jean Matsys, probably son of Quentin, who painted at a later date in the manner of his father.

Then again, the words "gold laces," which occur in a treaty of the fifteenth century between the town of Bruges and England, apply to laces in the sense of shoe-laces and cords for lacing up sleeves and dresses.

Séguin concludes : " As soon as Belgium acquired the art of pillow lace-making, she unremittingly applied herself to it, and in a short time converted it into a widespread industry, possessing well-merited reputation on account of the delicacy and beauty of its productions. All countries turned to her for them, and she became, as it were, the classic country of pillow lace. Credit for the invention of the special process was readily given to her, and no one has since taken the trouble to closely examine her title to it."

If as close an investigator as Madame Despierres could some day do for the history of Italian laces what she has done for that of Alençon laces, it seems quite probable that evidence would be forthcoming to corroborate what is at present a conjecture—that towards the year 1500 the north of Italy was the true cradle of the arts of pillow and needlepoint lace-making.

Meanwhile, and in the absence of anything more authentic, one may here repeat the pretty legend of Venice concerning pillow or bobbin lace-making.

"A young fisherman of the Adriatic was betrothed to a beautiful girl of one of the isles in the lagoon. Industrious as she was beautiful, the girl made a new net for her lover, who took it with him on board his boat. The first time he cast it into the sea he dragged therefrom an exquisite petrified wrack-grass, which he hastened to present to his *fiancée*.

"But war breaking out, the sailors and fishermen were pressed into the service of the Venetian navy, and departed for the East.

"The poor young girl wept at the departure of her lover, and for many days inconsolably contemplated his farewell gift to her. But whilst absorbed in following the wondrous and lovely ribs of the petrified wrack-grass, knitted together by the lightest of fibres, she began to twist and plait the threads weighted with small leads which hung around her net; little by little she wrought in a skilful manner a thread imitation of the beloved petrification, and thus was created the *merletti a piombini* (bobbin lace)!"

The story, if not true, is good: *Si non e vero e ben trovato.*

The most ancient mention, known at the present day, of bobbin lace in Italy, occurs in a deed, drawn up at Milan the 12th September, 1493, of assignment of property to two sisters, Angela and Ippolita Sforza, Visconti. One there reads of "*Una binda lavorata a poncto de doii fuxi par uno lenzolo*"—a band of work done with twelve bobbins to trim a sheet. The question of course arises, are these twelve bobbins early types of those which in later times were used by thousands of women for bobbin or pillow lace? Amongst other entries of the property given to the sisters Sforza is one of "*la mita de un fagotto quale aveva dentro certi designi da lavore le donne*"—half a scrap-book containing several drawings or patterns for ladies' work.

Here, again, is another piece of evidence—a collection of patterns preserved in the Royal Library at Munich, entitled *Neues modelbuch allerley gattungen Dantelschnür,* printed at Zurich by Christopher Froschowern, for all sorts of lace made and used in Germany, for the instruction of apprentices and other women working in Zurich and elsewhere; quarto in twenty-four sheets. On the title-page is a woodcut of two women making bobbin or pillow lace. Then follows a long preface, in which it is said: "Amongst the different arts we must not forget one which has been followed in our country for twenty-five years. Lace-making *was introduced in* 1536 *by merchants from Italy and Venice.* Many women seeing a means of livelihood in such work, quickly learned it, and reproduced lace with great skill. They first copied old patterns, but soon were enabled to invent new ones of great beauty. The industry spread itself about the country, and was carried to great perfection: it was found to be one specially suitable for women and brought in good profits. In the beginning these laces were used solely for trimming chemises and shirts; soon afterwards collars, trimmings for cuffs, caps, and fronts and bodies of dresses, for napkins, sheets, pillow-cases and coverlets, etc., were made in lace. Very soon such work was in great demand, and became an article of great luxury. Gold thread was subsequently introduced into some of it, and raised its value considerably; but this latter sort was attended with the inconvenience that it was more difficult to clean and wash than laces made with flax threads only."

This book of patterns establishes the facts that in 1536 Venice had for some years previously made lace, which had been exported, and that women in Germany and Switzerland had learned, from dealers coming from Venice, the way of making bobbin lace.

What occurred at Zurich also happened in other countries which had similar relations with Italy. Few countries were more closely connected, commercially and otherwise, with Italy than Belgium. Flemish artists flocked in numbers to study painting in Italy. Merchants or designers from Italy probably prompted the imparting of instruction in bobbin lace-making to the Flemings. And from the interest displayed by Flemish artists in this kind of lace Belgium soon assumed a first place as producer of it.

Quicherat tells us that towards the end of the fifteenth century it was the fashion in France to wear silken waistbands or girdles edged with a plaiting of meshes—called *bisette*. The name appears to have been derived from the colour of the silk, which was of brown-bread hue (*pain bis*), whence *bisette*; reminding us of another lace which similarly owes its name to its colour—namely, *blonde*. In the account of the entry of King Henry II. into Lyons on the 23rd September, 1548, we read that " the costumes were of velvet and satin, the humblest being of taffetas; some ornamented with gimp applications, others trimmed with *bisette* or with edgings of silver thread." A few years later, Elizabeth of France, on the occasion of her marriage with Philip II., made purchases in 1559 of "*bisette* and trimmings made with white thread of Florence."

Judging laces worn at the time by such portraits as that of Henry II. at Versailles (the earliest French painting in which lace is depicted), it will be seen that they were of no greater importance than that belonging to the sisters Sforza-Visconti, which was made with twelve bobbins. The collar of the king is in fact trimmed with a tiny dentated edging of open work.

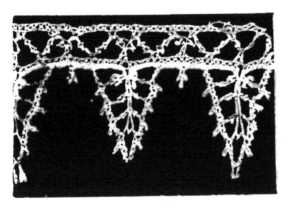

Fig. 121.—A bobbin or pillow-made *passement* of the sixteenth century.

The name *passement* (also used in England in the sixteenth century), was given to the earliest plaited thread laces or bobbin laces (see figs. 121 and 122). It comes from the title of the corporation of *Passementiers*, who had the monopoly, according to their statutes of 1663 (article 21), "of making all sorts of passements of lacework on the pillow, with bobbins, pins, and by hand" (probably in this case with a hooked or crochet needle), "in gold and silver thread, both real and false, in silk, and white and coloured thread." In the accounts of the king's treasurer, 1557 (*Archives Nationales.*, KK., 106), appears, "Passement of fine black silk *dentellé* (with open dentations) on one side."

The accounts of the Queen of Navarre (1577) also

show an entry : " For two ells of silver passement with deep dentations (*haute dantelle*), to be used as a facing, at sixty *solz* the ell." *

An inventory (1645) of the Church of St. Médard, at Paris, has mention of "four lengths of fine cambric to surround the pulpit, and a beautiful surplice for the preacher, trimmed with deep *passements à dantelle*."

Hence *passement* and *dentelle* are convertible terms for bobbin lace, or open work trimmings of plaited and twisted thread.

As we have stated, the *passementiers* or trimming makers often used gimp cord. For bobbin work this gimp cord, from its stiffness, could only be used in respect of large open passements. Whence the name of guipure came to be used for all lace in which the grounds were very large and of irregular openings.

Bobbin laces, of less elaborate pattern than needle-point laces, were cheaper, and gladly welcomed for use by such as could not afford the expense of point lace.

Further, as Charles Blanc so justly says, " When ruffs or gadrooned (pleated) collars were imported from Italy, the needlepoint laces with which some would be trimmed presented a hard appearance, converting the encircling ornament of the neck into a sort of collar bristling with sharp points. But when these stiff guipures were superseded by bobbin laces, these lighter and more supple articles softened the contours which they trimmed, and almost gave a vaporous effect to the cut-out shapes of the triple-staged

* *Archives Nationales*, KK., 162.

ruffs imprisoning the heads of their wearers " *
(fig. 123).

As rapidly as the industry of pillow lace-making
passed into various countries, so, as we have seen in
the case of Switzerland, each locality specialized it in
some manner, that various characteristic laces were
accordingly produced, and came to be identified with
their native places.

In Italy, Milan and Genoa were two principal towns
in which pillow lace
was extensively
made, whilst Venice
remained the chief
centre for needle-
points. Very fre-
quently the less
complicated of the
patterns for needle-
made laces were
adapted and repro-
duced by the pillow-

Fig. 122.—Bobbin or pillow-made
passement (*Musée des Arts décoratifs.*)

lace makers. Gradually, however, the more skilful
of the pattern designers of whom Isabetta Catanea
Parasole is an instance, invented patterns for pillow
laces, marking under them the number of bobbins to be
used in working each.

In Saxony Dame Barbara Etterlein, wife of Christopher Uttmann, a great proprietor of mines, living
in the castle of St. Annaberg, introduced the industry
of pillow lace-making to the wives of the miners, as
a means of profit for the family purse. A story is

* Charles Blanc, *l'Art dans la Parure,* p. 291.

told of an old woman—somewhat of a sorceress, no
doubt—who, noticing the kindly devotion of the good
Châtelaine of St. Annaberg in instructing the poor
peasant women to make pillow lace, foretold that
St. Anne would reward her in making her children

Fig. 123.– Portrait attributed to Van Mierevelt, 1568—1641
(belonging to M. G. Duplessis).

prosper, in allowing none to die during her lifetime,
and in multiplying their descendants so that they
should be as numerous as the bobbins in the district.
The prediction was approximately verified, since, on
her death in 1575, Barbara Uttmann left sixty-five
children and grandchildren.

In Spain, fine and rich fabrics made at the different *hôtels des Tiraz* were greatly esteemed ; and silk and gold and silver thread passements were freely produced to adorn them. These passements were for a long time known under the name of Spanish points (*Points d'Espagne*), on account of the admirable workmanship displayed in them. *Finesse* was not perhaps so marked a quality in them as that of glittering and massive effect. This characteristic makes it easy to distinguish a *Point d'Espagne* when one happens to meet with it (fig. 124).

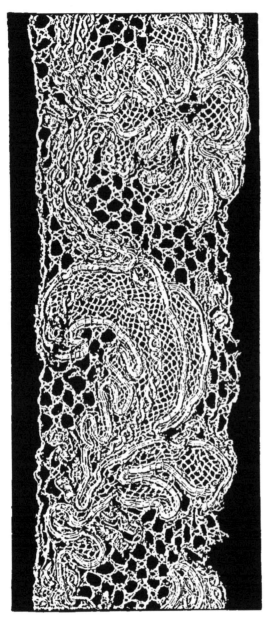

Fig. 124.—Pillow lace of gold and silk thread made in Spain (*Point d'Espagne*).

Belgium and Holland were noted, not for pillow laces made with silk, gold and silver thread, but for those made with delicate flax threads. In those countries the best linens of the world were woven ; with threads of similar material were made the very fine laces for trimming broad collars and great linen cuffs, which are to be seen in the Flemish portraits of the period * (fig. 125). The designs for such laces were distinct from the Italian patterns, and were usually composed of devices derived from the local flora. These departures and improvements raised Flanders to the front rank as a pillow lace-making country.

Whilst the French Court enriched itself with both Italian and Flemish laces, its humbler followers contented themselves with laces of less pretence. The farmer's wife trimmed her caps and the townsfolk their dresses with laces called *mignonnette, campane,* and *gueuse*—the latter a very popular passement—all of which play a part in the Revolt of the Laces (*Révolte des Passements*), already cited, and were made in considerable quantities in the suburbs of Paris. The greater part of these smaller laces were rigid, without much ornamental design in them, and it is scarcely fitting to mention them in a treatise which proposes in the main to deal with the artistic side of lace-making.

Of the French provinces where pillow lace-making was soonest established as an industry the Auvergne is the first in age.

Many of the men there were employed as carriers—an occupation of considerable importance before good highways and the means of wheel traffic were known. These hardy mountaineers, travelling by short stages, with packs on their backs, undertook long journeys, and storing themselves in the Midi with costly merchan-

---

* *Histoire de la Peinture Hollandaise,* by Henry Havard, p. 72.

dize like silks and laces, which are easily portable,
would come to Paris and the north of France to find

Fig. 125.—Portrait of a courtier of the period of Louis XIII.
(after Abraham Bosse).

markets for them.   Thus, no doubt, they returned
to their native districts with intelligence of the new

industry of pillow lace-making, in the produce of which considerable trade flourished between Paris and Italy. The women of the Auvergne set themselves to imitate these new wares, which in course of time their husbands took off to sell,—selling them with good profit on their line of journey here and there, and often at great fairs like those of Beaucaire and Guibray, where places in the *fosse aux toiles* were assigned to the itinerant lace vendors.

The same sort of dissemination of knowledge about lace-making and of traffic in its wares took place in Lorraine, whence, in 1615, Claude Gelée, a young man, afterwards surnamed Le Lorrain, travelled into Italy in company with his uncle, a carrier and dealer in laces, who was anxious to get his nephew instructed in the art of painting, for which he displayed precocious predilection.

Aurillac and Le Puy-en-Velay were the chief centres of lace-making in the Auvergne. Gold and silver laces were made principally at Aurillac, and were exported in great quantities to Spain, where the consumption of such goods often exceeded the home production. Le Puy, however, was more noted for thread laces and silk guipures.

The lace industry was found to be of much profit by the numerous families adopting it; and when its development and the accompanying prosperity were menaced through sumptuary edicts, public feeling ran high against them.

Outdoing the edict of Louis XIII., passed in 1629, which permitted " a consumption of laces provided they were manufactured in the kingdom at a cost not exceeding three livres the ell for insertion and edging," the

Parliament of Toulouse issued a decree which the Seneschal of Le Puy made known in 1639 to the sound of the trumpet throughout the town, and was severer than the king's. This decree forbade, under penalty of a heavy fine, "everybody of either sex, quality, or condition from wearing any sort of lace, whether of silk or white thread with glittering passement of gold or silver, real or false." This naturally produced consternation amongst the inhabitants of Le Puy ; and well-nigh annihilated the industry throughout the province. At this juncture a Jesuit Father, since canonized by the Church as St. François Régis, appeared as a preacher in Le Puy and in Auvergne, distributing wherever he went pious advice and charitable relief so effectually as to lighten the unhappy effects of the decree. Moved by the sufferings and lamentations of women reduced to misery, he said, " Have confidence ; pray to God to help me, and lace-making shall not perish !" Then taking his departure for Toulouse, he interceded with much fervour in favour of the Auvergnese lace-workers, and obtained from the local Parliament a revocation in the following year, 1640, of its cruel decree. In addition he commended to the tender protection of his religious brethren —Spanish Jesuits--the lace-workers who carried their laces for sale to the southern side of the Pyrenees. Trade and prosperity revived, and to this day the lace-makers of the Auvergne invoke St. François Régis as their patron saint.

That consummate connoisseur of gems, fine stones, and *objets d'art*, Cardinal Mazarin, held the Aurillac laces in high appreciation. These laces are frequently mentioned in the inventory of the property he left at his death in 1661. "The doublet and breeches of scarlet cloth belonging to Mons. le Cardinal are bordered with red and black silk laces."

The *Mercure Galant*, giving a description of a masked ball, says that " the Prince de Conti wore a mantle of Point d'Aurillac of gold and silver;" the Duchesse de Mortemart "wore below her plumes a veil of silver Aurillac lace falling over her shoulders;" whilst the Marquis de Colbert, as an African, had "long hanging sleeves bordered with gold Aurillac laces."

The king, Louis XIV., wore a costume made by his tailor, Claude Hochar, of black brocaded with gold flowers, for which he paid thirteen hundred livres, and which consisted of doublet, breeches, shoes, cloak, and gloves, all bordered with silk guipure."

Under such excellent patronage it is easy to understand why in the *Révolte des Passements* Aurillac laces are represented as being so accustomed to perfumed saloons, that they hesitate about returning to their mountain homes to be used probably for no better purpose than for tying up Roquefort cheeses!

Early pillow laces were comparatively narrow; throughout Italy, France, Spain, and Flanders, they were made in strips on the pillow, the bobbins hanging in one and the same direction. When the demand for wider trimmings arose, increased width of lace was obtained by adding a passement or dentated border to the band—" *bande et passement.*" In the sixteenth century similar means were resorted to. But in the seventeenth century the making of wide laces was attempted. . Then arose the question of how to divide

and distribute the work for facility of execution. In
Italy, France, and Spain large pieces of lace were
made by dividing the pattern into horizontal bands,

Fig. 126.—Louis XIV. when a child, after a portrait by Mignard.

the pieces of which could be stitched together. In
Belgium another means was invented ; this consisted
of dividing the pattern, not by bands, but into small

and separate pieces, the boundaries of which coincided with the capricious curves of flowers, leaves, or other ornaments in the pattern, after the manner of dividing up needlepoint lace patterns. This ingenious division, whereby the distribution of a single large pattern could be effected in numberless small pieces, was to a large extent a cause of the great success which attended the Belgian industry. By working each *motif* of a pattern independently, the union of the separate pieces together became a more certain and successful operation, especially when each happened to be of rich and complicated work. Instead of *passements* like those of Italy and France, in which the open parts dominated around slender and thin devices of patterns, the Flemish bethought them of a totally different character of lace. They gave greater attention to the making of the close portions, obtaining richer contrasts between them and the adjoining parts rendered in open stitches. The compact work in the floral designs assimilated admirably with the wide flat linen collars which were fashionable in Flanders. This fashion passed over to France; and under Louis XIII. the wide flat collar (see figs. 125 and 126) superseded the pleated ruffs, the edgings of which had been the means of creating a reputation for the *punti in aere* and the Italian passements (or *merletti à piombini*). Flemish *guipures* therefore mark a progress in the making of pillow laces, and deservedly enjoyed a success. Up to the death of Mazarin, Louis XIV. himself wore nothing but *rabats* (or bands falling over the chest from below the chin) of pillow-lace guipures, to which several portraits of the young king by Mignard testify. It

was only at the age of twenty-five, and at the suggestion of Colbert, who had succeeded Mazarin, that the
king took to wearing Venetian needlepoints. Two or
three years later he thought of having them reproduced
by French skill.

In the course of the seventeenth century, laces with
meshed grounds or nets (*réseaux*) were first made in
Belgium. These were produced by much the same
methods as those for the Flemish *guipures*, and
often after the same patterns, with modifications in
the grounds only. But by a strange anomaly such
laces, although made in the same way and in the same
country, were variously called *guipures de Flandres*
when bars or tyes were introduced between the
ornamental devices, or *dentelles* or *Points d'Angleterre*
when meshed grounds were used instead of bars or
tyes.

Many explanations have been offered as to the
variation in naming these laces. England no doubt
has made lace, but all the world knows that she has
sold a much larger quantity than she herself ever produced. She imported them from Belgium, and sold
them to France and elsewhere, giving them her own
name, and not that of the country of their origin. Mrs.
Palliser explains what took place thus:

"The English, close neighbours of the Flemish, were
amongst the first to appreciate the beautiful laces made
by the latter. From the seventeenth century England
consumed an immense quantity of Flemish laces; and
when those with meshed grounds made their appearance she literally monopolized the wearing of them.
But extravagance in this direction provoked, as it did

in France, the issue of sumptuary edicts. In 1662 the English Parliament, alarmed at the sums of money expended on foreign point, and desirous to protect the English bone lace manufacture, passed an Act prohibiting the importation of all foreign lace. The English lace-merchants, at a loss how to supply the Brussels point required at the court of Charles II., invited Flemish lace-makers to settle in England and there establish the manufacture. The scheme, however, was unsuccessful : England did not produce the necessary flax, and the lace made was inferior in quality. The merchants therefore adopted a more simple expedient. Possessed of large capital, they bought up the choicest laces of the Brussels market, and then smuggling them over to England, sold them under the name of *Points d'Angleterre*, or 'English Point.' The account of the seizure made by the Marquis de Nesmond of a vessel laden with Flanders lace, bound for England, in 1678, will afford some idea of the extent to which this smuggling was carried on. The cargo comprised 744,953 ells of lace, without enumerating handkerchiefs, collars, fichus, aprons, petticoats, fans, gloves, etc., all of the same material. From this period, *Point de Bruxelles* became more and more unknown, and was at last effaced by *Point d'Angleterre*, a name it still retains."

What seems evident from this, is that the name *Points d'Angleterre* was adopted, not for the *Guipures de Flandres* already known in England and passing as English laces, but for the newly invented laces with meshed grounds.

Another explanation, and possibly a more logical

one, might be that English pillow lace-makers may have made laces with meshed grounds. These becoming the vogue, the English supply may have been inadequate to the demand, and so the English dealers had recourse to Flemish labour in the production of similar laces, which would be termed "*Points d'Angleterre à réseaux.*"

"*Une grande dentelle d'Angleterre*" is spoken of in the *Révolte des Passements* (1661). In all inventories of the period entries of such lace occur: the *Mercure Galant* often mentions it, and goes so far as to say, in 1678, that "corsage and sleeves were bordered with a white and delicate lace, which undoubtedly came from the best lace-making centres in England."

The earliest *Points d'Angleterre* were made in separate pieces, each, however, consisting of ornament and meshed ground. Later, however, the subdivision of labour was increased. The flower (fig. 146) or ornament alone was made by certain hands, whilst others would be employed in making bands of net or meshed ground, on which the flowers were *appliqués* or stitched with a needle. This class of lace was called *application d'Angleterre.* It is not quite determined whether this lace was made towards the end of the seventeenth or in the succeeding century. On this point we shall have more to say in the next chapter.

, When Colbert founded the Royal Manufactory in 1665, at the Hôtel de Beaufort, Paris, he directed the head administration to arrange for the making "of all sorts of threadwork, both with the needle and with bobbins on the pillow," in the various selected centres. But if this experiment was less successful in respect of bobbin laces than of needlepoint laces, the making of the two sorts has a bearing on the history of bobbin or pillow lace-making which is of importance and cannot be ignored. Besides, has not Voltaire told us that whilst two hundred head lace-makers were induced to come from the Netherlands into France, not more than thirty came from Venice?

The French towns in which lace-making was organized as an industry were numerous; some, no doubt, achieved little or no success with it; and one never hears now of the lace-making efforts of Rheims, Auxerre, Loudun, La Flèche, Le Mans,—all of which, however, are mentioned in Colbert's Correspondence, which reveals the minister's close interest in the fortunes of the industry he so warmly promoted. Of the towns materially benefited by his energy and encouragement, we may name above others Aurillac, Arras, and Le Quesnoy.

The latter town is probably unknown to most of our readers as one famed for its lace-making. This, however, is accounted for by its having been supplanted in the eighteenth century by its better-known neighbour, Valenciennes. The invention of Valenciennes laces, amongst the most esteemed of bobbin or pillow laces, is undoubtedly a development of the lace-making operations founded at Le Quesnoy by Colbert. On its first appearance in the seventeenth century little was said about Valenciennes lace; and, as we shall further on show, it was not until the following century that it became famous.

The first Norman centre of lace-making was Havre; and as early as 1661 Havre laces were known and are referred to in the *Révolte des Passements.* In 1692 the Governor, M. de St. Aignan, gave a great impulse to the Havre industry, in which some twenty thousand fisherwomen or peasants of Caux were engaged. The Duc de Penthièvre, who lived at the Château d'Eu, was also a leading patron of this pillow lace-making.

Paris was affected by the general movement initiated by Louis XIV. and Colbert. Apart from the offices of the royal lace manufactories, at the Hôtel de Beaufort in Paris, rooms for lace-workers were provided in the Château de Madrid,* in the Bois de Boulogne, principally for pillow lace-makers. Their influence extended to the Ile-de-France, where, according to the Marquis de la Gomberdière, " the children of ten thousand families were taught to make laces." Chantilly also dates its lace manufacture from this time.

The *Point de Paris* was a somewhat common little lace, made in the *Faubourg St. Antoine.* And on this account, no doubt, the Comte de Marsan, youngest son of the Comte d'Harcourt, fixed upon this quarter of the town as the more suitable in which to find lodgings for his former nurse, a Madame Dumont of Brussels. He obtained from the king a licence for her to employ all the pillow lace-makers there. Assisted by her four daughters, Madame Dumont supervised nearly two hundred of the lace-workers in the suburb. Her management was attended with such prosperity that she determined to transfer her workwomen to a more central place. She accordingly placed them in one or

* A silk stocking manufactory also found accommodation in the Château de Madrid.

other of the numerous buildings which formed the Hôtel de Chaumont, situated in the Rue St. Denis and the Rue St. Sauveur. Whether it was from the great and unnecessary size of the hôtel buildings, or what, Madame Dumont's prosperity did not follow her here ; and shortly after she took her departure for Portugal to establish a lace-making centre there, leaving the direction of the manufactory in the Hôtel de Chaumont to Mdlle. de Marsan.

The *Livre Commode; or, Addresses in the City of Paris*, by Pradel, published in 1692, shows that the lace-makers during the reign of Louis XIV. occupied work-rooms, near the beginning of the Rue St. Honoré, between the Place aux Chats and the Piliers des Halles. Two streets intersected it,—the Rue des Bourdonnais, in which silk laces were specially sold ; and the Rue de Béthisy where points and thread laces were sold.

Summary.—The details given in the foregoing pages indicate that the demand for bobbin or pillow laces began to display itself very little later than that for needlepoint laces, and that in the seventeenth century the manufacture of them sprang up in different places. The success of pillow lace-making in the first periods of its life was not as great as that of needle-point lace-making. Venice and Alençon reigned supreme in the latter industry. Some years intervened before pillow lace-making rose in public estimation, and was called upon to interpret designs of artistic character. Many of the now better-known places, like Valenciennes, Mechlin, Chantilly, had enjoyed no reputation in the earlier days of pillow lace-making. Colbert neverthe-less had well prepared the soil ; in the north, as in the centre, of the country, from Arras and Le Quesnoy to Aurillac and Loudun, he had spread a network of instruction, and had sown seeds which were destined to bear fruit.

Belgium, through the invaluable aid of English trade, began to find outlets to all countries for the produce of her lace industry, and infused into pillow laces special technical characteristics which have not since been superseded. Their development, in many branches, belongs to the reign of Louis XV., when, as we shall see, filmy and supple pillow laces flourished in an extraordinary manner, whilst needlepoint laces appear to have been stricken with a sort of decadence after the death of the Grand Monarque.

Whilst, then, the apogee of the needlepoint method of making laces is in the seventeenth century, that of the bobbin or pillow process belongs to the eigh-. teenth century.

CHAPTER II.

FROM LOUIS XV. TO THE PRESENT TIME.

PILLOW laces have preserved those well-marked characteristics which are to be observed in specimens made at the beginning of the eighteenth century. Instead of their patterns being, as they were at first, imitations of those for needlepoint laces, a new departure was made when patterns were designed to meet the peculiar requirements of the bobbin or pillow method of manufacture. Woman's coquetry, cultivated to its utmost limits during a century of elegance, whetted keenness of perception in initiating all the effects which were possible with such supple and diaphanous tissues, soft and yielding to the touch, graceful in folds, and ethereal in filminess, as were procurable from dainty twistings and plaitings done with bobbins. Hence arose that series of charming productions known respectively as Valenciennes, Mechlin, Angleterre, Chantilly, and Blonde laces, each of which possesses individuality of style. In attempting to describe them, we hope to demonstrate their right to the reputation which they have inherited down to the present time.

Foregoing chronological order in our remarks upon these laces, we hope to avoid much repetition which would be inevitable were we to deal with these laces by historic periods analogous to those touched upon in describing embroidery and needlepoint laces. At the same time, it is but right to say that this plan of proceeding cannot but be somewhat incomplete, since little short of a separate volume would suffice for fully setting forth all the variety of details to be found in these typical classes of pillow lace. Our remarks will therefore be limited to generic types of pillow lace, to one

Fig. 127.—*Guipure* of Le Puy, also called Cluny lace.

or the other of which other pillow laces are nearly related.

Passement.—The oldest class of bobbin or pillow lace is, as we have previously stated, that of *passements*, the light and open *guipures* figured in the pattern books. The making of these has not ceased since its commencement early in the sixteenth century. From being somewhat spasmodic, and undertaken by few women, the industry became localized in different parts of France, particularly Le Puy and at Mirecourt.

The Auvergne has ever since retained its celebrity as a classic home of *guipures* made in bands, for which designs of geometric character, with *motifs* like squares, stars, and formal blossoms, have been and continue to be chiefly used. The great number of women engaged in this industry, the simplicity of their life in the mountains, and its modest requirements, have helped to make this local lace-making the most important in the world. In 1851 Felix Aubry computed from official returns that upwards of 130,000 women were then

Fig. 128.—*Passement* in fine thread (Le Puy or Mirecourt).

engaged in it. Thread *passements*, as shown in fig. 122, have always been made by them. From time to time fashion discards, whilst at others it favours these *passements*, as was recently the case when a demand for *Guipures de Cluny* arose (fig. 127). This purely fanciful name was adopted from the Musée de Cluny, where samples of ancient laces are preserved.

But that which has tended more than anything else to the perpetuation of the industry, is the versatility of the Auvergnese workers in using with equal facility variety of threads. As circumstances require, flax, silk, worsted, goat's hair, and Angora rabbit hair threads are employed. Black *guipures* (figs. 129 and 130), in the production of which the industry has for a great part of the present century been engaged, are made with a rich and strong silk thread. These certainly reflect more honour upon the lace-making of Le Puy than any other kinds of kindred work made there; and it is perhaps surprising that they do not keep a longer hold upon public taste. No where have better woollen laces been made than in the Auvergne. Somewhat thick in texture and bold in pattern, they nevertheless harmonize admirably when used as trimmings to dresses made of similar material.

Fig. 129.—Black silk *guipure* (Le Puy).

Gold and silver laces long famous at Aurillac continue to be made in the Auvergne.

Fig. 130.—Flounce of black silk *guipure* (in the museum of Le Puy).

Craponne is notable for its furniture stout thread *guipures* of low price.

Mirecourt in the Vosges makes a similar lace to

that of Le Puy, but rather finer in quality. The workmanship is careful and the patterns are well chosen. Considerable efforts have been put forward to develop this class of lace-making which has existed for so long in Lorraine, but the double competition of the Auvergne on the one hand, and Belgium on the other, in each of which a far larger number of lace-makers are at work, has often pressed the Lorraine industry sorely ; still it maintains its reputation as one of the best directed branches in 'respect of artistic aim (fig. 128).

In Italy, Genoa has remained faithful to the production of well-made *guipures* with small blossom or seed devices but rather gross in quality. A characteristic which is noticed in the *Révolte des passements* when the *Point de Gênes* is spoken of as having a too stout substance ("*le corps un peu gros*"). Black silk *guipures* made in the villages of the seaboard are very much of the same nature as those made in Malta.

No matter what may be the class of material used in respect of the threads and their size, the make of all these *guipures* accords with that of the primitive *passements;* the patterns, on the whole, are geometric, and the work is made in bands.

Point de Milan.—Milan, after first making *passements*, adopted patterns of flowing scrolls and blossoming flowers, after the style of the Venetian points *à foliami.* In these we have another sort of *guipure*, the leading feature of which is the bold flowing scroll devices. These undoubtedly lacked the rich reliefs which abounded in the Venetian needlepoint laces of similar ornamental *motifs :* the flowers in this Milanese lace were flat and wrought with the appearance of compactly woven linen ; here and there, somewhat sparsely, would be introduced open fillings (*à jours*), or else small holes would be left to lighten the tape-like effect of the close work. At the same time, the plaited bars or tyes used as a ground to the earlier patterns very admirably set

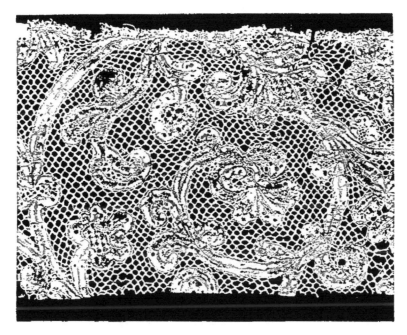

Fig. 131.—Milanese pillow lace with mesh ground.

off the curved and scrolled devices. As in the Venetian points, eagles, armorial bearings, and crowns were frequently intermingled with them.

Unfortunately the taste for grounds of small meshes carried all before it in the eighteenth century ; and although characteristic scrolls and flowers were still used in patterns, they were not so effective in contrast with the meshed grounds (figs. 131 and 132) as they had been with the bars or tyes of the *guipures.* Genoa imitated Milan; and Venice herself did the same in respect of those of her pillow laces which were made in the island of Palestrina and Chioggia. A distinctiveness, however, belongs to the *Points de Milan* as a class of pillow-made laces.*

A version of these Milanese laces has been produced by using tape for the scroll forms and flowers, and filling in the open portions, between the tapes, with needle-point stitches.

Fig. 132.—Milanese pillow lace with mesh ground, eighteenth century (the property of Madame Franck).

Belgium, as already stated, was the earliest of lace-making countries to free herself from Italian influence in the matters of make and pattern, and to strike out an independent path. The development of the *Point de Flandres* about the period of Louis XIII. has been sketched. The style of its patterns was flowery and rich, somewhat heavy in detail, of very flat work (fig. 126), notable for delicate veinings composed of

* This industry is still kept up round about the little town of Cantu in the province of Milan.

pinholes to lighten with happy effect the close white surfaces. Comparatively primitive as this style is, it nevertheless contains the germs of the later and varied productions we now propose to allude to.

Valenciennes Lace.—This did not acquire a distinctive appellation until the eighteenth century; it will be remembered that the centre of the manufacture

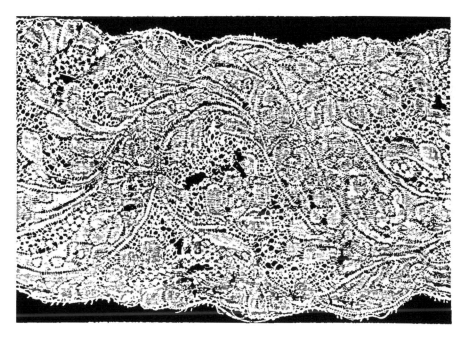

Fig. 133.—Valenciennes lace with "snowy ground" (*fond de neige*).

at the time of Colbert was Le Quesnoy. But the Flemish mistresses of the craft clearly instructed the workers there to produce flat and closely made pillow lace such as we have described. This make of lace, especially in respect of floral and other ornamental details, survives throughout various phases of what is known as Valenciennes lace. The modifications, which gave birth to the features of these various phases, applied to the grounds and portions intervening between the floral and ornamental devices. Little by little the intervening spaces were enlarged and subjected to different treatments. The small bars or tyes, to be noted in the prototypes of Valenciennes laces, were superseded by groupings of dots or pea forms which, in dainty white thread intertwistings, assumed the appearance of orderly sprinklings of snow-flakes, whence Valenciennes laces in which these grounds occurred were spoken of, as in the *Révolte des passe-*

Fig. 134.—Valenciennes lace, seventeenth century (in the *Musée des Arts décoratifs*).

ments, as *Escadrons de Neige* (Squadrons of Snow) (fig. 133).

After divers variations (fig. 134) in the making of grounds, the classic meshed ground, with which the name of Valenciennes has since become identified, was developed. In this the mesh is square or diamond shape, of great regularity, very open, and each side of it is of closely plaited threads (fig. 135). Both floral ornament and ground of meshes are worked together with the same quality of thread. The ornament is not picked out with any outline of thread, as is the case with Mechlin lace (see fig. 139); and the absence of such thread or of any work in the nature of relief, conduces to facility in successfully washing Valenciennes lace, which, of all laces, is most easily ironed and suitable for being "got up" with linen.

The elegant dishabilles of duchesses and marchionesses in the eighteenth century were bedecked with exquisite laces of this sort; their light flowery patterns, very delicately veined in the fine filmy parts, were agreeably set off by the intervening grounds of diamond-shaped meshes, which formed a dainty trellis-

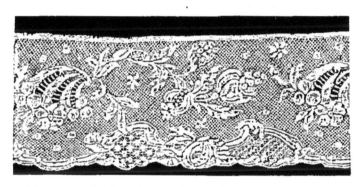

Fig. 135.—Valenciennes lace (eighteenth century).

work about them.   These laces certainly justified their reputation.

Up to the period of the Revolution, the town of Valenciennes had been the centre of this particular industry.   Its name has always been associated with it, notwithstanding that for some time lace-making has disappeared from the town itself.   The industry is now carried on in two provinces of Belgium.   Almost all the convents for poor girls, and the *béguinages*, where widows and spinsters congregate in communities, make Valenciennes laces.   Along the line between Poperinghe, Courtrai, and Ghent an active commerce in these laces is carried on ; the town of Ypres makes a better quality (fig. 136).

In France, Valenciennes laces are made at the small frontier town of Bailleul, where a museum of laces has been established. Valenciennes and other large towns have, however, taken no trouble to preserve the smallest specimen of the fabrics which made their names famous.

Fig. 136.—Modern Valenciennes (Ypres) lace, with square mesh ground.

During the last thirty years a lace termed Valenciennes-Brabant has been made, in which the division of labour, common to Flemish laces, has been adopted. Instead of being made in one piece, as is the case with Valenciennes lace, the flowers and ornaments are made first and the groundwork is then inserted between them. This process is well adapted to the production of large pieces which could not be conveniently produced in narrow bands or strips of lace (fig. 137).

Mechlin Lace.—This is a light-looking lace, the close

portions of the ornament and flowers, etc., being more

Fig. 137.—Flounce of Valenciennes-Brabant lace.

filmy than those in Valenciennes laces. It is indeed
the most supple of all laces; but a more distinguishing

feature in it is the fine bright thread which outlines all
the ornamental shapes in it.   Before the meshed ground,
ultimately adopted as the more suitable, was decided on,
various attempts and experiments were made, as in the
case of the Valenciennes ground, and amongst these a
notable snow ground (*fond de neige*, see fig. 138) sur-

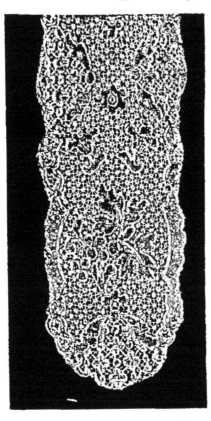

vived for some time.   At
length, however, a normal
type of ground with small
hexagonal meshes, some-
what resembling that of
Brussels pillow lace, only
with shorter plaited sides
to each mesh, was adopted.
It is without question the
prettiest of all pillow-made
grounds.   Mechlin lace was
in great request during the
reign of Louis XV., and
the *rococo* style of ornament
prevailed in its designs.   To
some extent in their lightness and transparence they
may be compared with similar patterns upon contemporary engraved glasses from

Fig. 138.—Lappet of Mechlin lace
"snowy ground" (*fond de neige*).

Saxony and Bohemia (fig. 139).   Under Louis XVI.
floral sprays and delicate interlacings which gave oppor-
tunities for varieties of fillings (*à jours*) were used in
the patterns.   Later on, the patterns consisted of
orderly scatterings of tiny blossoms, spots, and so forth,
which make a pleasing play of effect in contrast with

the regularity of the meshed grounds. No better lace can be found to assimilate with, and adorn, light textures such as gauze and muslin. It is admirably suited for *barbes* and headdresses, and our grandmothers showed cunning appreciation of its appropriateness in bedecking their undulating mounds of white hair.

The district between Mechlin, Antwerp, and Louvain has always been celebrated for its make of Mechlin lace.

Lille and Arras laces are somewhat of the same

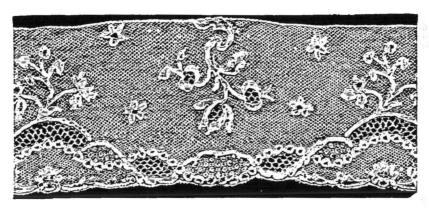

Fig. 139.—Mechlin lace (eighteenth century).

character; the principal difference between them and Mechlin being in the less elaborated make of their grounds, in which the meshes are made by twisting, not plaiting, threads; the other portions of the lace are of the same make as Mechlin.

In the country about Bayeux, laces, having a close affinity to Mechlin lace, are manufactured with fine thread. Important pieces for *fichus*, *mantillas*, or head scarves, coming from this district, have all the suppleness and softness which contribute to the seductive charm of this class of lace (fig. 140).

Chantilly. — Chantilly, in the seventeenth century,

became the rallying point of the lace-makers from the Ile-de-France. After producing lace of modest artistic pretension, such as *gueuse* and the *Point de Paris*, which latter was a sort of second-rate Mechlin or Valenciennes type of lace, Chantilly suddenly achieved a reputation by making silk laces, especially those in black silk.

Fig. 140.—White thread pillow lace (Bayeux).

Specimens of old Chantilly lace, whether of white or black silk, are remarkable for patterns in which are introduced vases and flowery baskets similar in shape and decoration to those made in Chantilly pottery, which were highly esteemed at the same time as Chantilly lace (fig. 141).

The material employed for the Chantilly black laces is a silk termed *grenadine d'Alais*. The peculiar twist in spinning these silk threads diminishes the brilliant silkiness of the unspun material, and persons frequently imagine that Chantilly black lace is therefore made with black flax. The earliest form of mesh in Chantilly lace grounds is a lozenge, crossed at its two opposite points by horizontal threads. Grounds with meshes of this description are termed *fonds chant*, an abbreviation of the name Chantilly (fig. 142). The fillings introduced into the flowers and other ornaments in Chantilly lace are of mesh grounds of old date, which, according to the districts where they were made, are called *vitré*, *marriage*, or *cinq trous*. Chantilly, however, less than its sister centres of manufacture, withstood the temptation of imitating the mesh common to Alençon grounds, which for a long time has been employed in almost all other black laces.

Black lace, however, has not been in such general demand as white laces. That it possesses characteristic charm, and is peculiarly suitable for the wear of ladies of a certain age, few will be disposed to deny. As Directress of St. Cyr, Madame de Maintenon, always wore Chantilly black lace. For shawls and ample

Fig. 141.—Chantilly lace (eighteenth century).

scarves, for mantles and other articles of outdoor costume, black lace is probably without a rival.

After, as it were, making the fortune of Chantilly and the neighbouring districts as far as Gisors, for many years, the black lace industry disappeared from the suburbs of Paris, to be revived in Normandy about Caen and Bayeux, where, during the present century, it has been extensively followed. According to Felix Aubry, upwards of sixty thousand workers are there engaged in it at their homes. It has become a valuable auxiliary means of livelihood in a district almost wholly dependent upon agriculture. Such patient application as is indispensable in its practice, involving the constant use of a large number of bobbins, is rarely to be met with amongst dwellers in the vicinity of a great city like Paris.

The make of Normandy black laces has been carried to a higher condition than previously attained anywhere else. Patterns in which flowers and ornamental *motifs* are rendered with the utmost delicacy of gradation in texture have been produced with the greatest

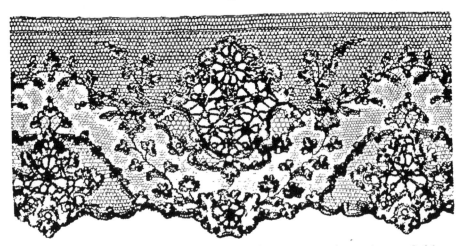

Fig. 142.—Chantilly black lace with the grounds interchanged (the *fond chant* and the imitation Alençon ground).

success at Bayeux, and defy all comparison with the earlier Chantilly laces. This specialty in gradation of texture pertains to modern black lace, and is unknown in old laces of a cognate class (fig. 143).

The towns of Grammont and Enghien in Belgium also produce black laces, which may be distinguished from French work by being less elaborated in changeful *nuances* or gradations : the threads to indicate veinings of leaves have no delicate open work about them like that to be seen in the French black lace.

Fig. 143.—Black lace lappet (Bayeux).

Blonde, or white silk pillow lace.—Certain sorts of pillow-made laces derive their names from some characteristic of the material with which they are made, instead of from the town of their manufacture. Such, for instance, is *blonde*, which is one of the more important types we shall mention. Originally, *blonde* was made with unbleached silk, the pale straw colour of which gave rise to its name. *Bisette* is another lace which, in the sixteenth century, was so called in consequence of the colour of the thread with which it was made. But *blonde* is now made only with white and black silk. Two different sizes of thread are employed in its manufacture, a fine one for the meshed ground, and a coarser and more fluffy one for the ornament.

Early patterns for *blonde* show but few details of close work (*mat*), the ornament being principally in outline wrought sinuously with a single thread, thereby producing a diversity of interlacing open forms. This style, much affected in the eighteenth century, was adopted at Caen towards 1840, when quantities of such work was produced (fig. 144).

Marie Antoinette's predilection for *blonde* of this description is well known; the book of her dress-maker (Madame Eloffe)* gives evidence of it on almost every page. The patterns she affected were thin and poor in effect; but it is well to note the distinction between the elegancies of the first years of her reign and the almost sad simplicities of the later years, as exhibited in fashions adopted by this Queen who under-went cruel fluctuations of fortunes. It was during her

* Comte de Reiset, *Reproduction du livre journal de Madame Eloffe,* published by Didot.

later years that Marie Antoinette wore considerable quantities of the light patterned *blonde* laces.

Since then, *blonde* has been more frequently made in the Spanish style, with big flowery *motifs* wrought in excellent close work (*mats*), sheeny as satin, and standing out in vigorous contrast with the delicate net ground (fig. 145). Occasionally, spaces, filled in (*grillés*)

Fig. 144.—Light *blonde* of white silk (Caen).

with thin silk thread, alternate with the compact parts of flat and stouter silken thread ; this variety is termed *Blonde mi-genre.*

The mantilla, the national headdress of Spanish women in Europe and America, is made in both sorts of *blonde, blondes mates* and *blondes mi-genres;* the Mexican and Havannah patterns being bolder and heavier than the European Spanish ones. Unfortunately the

Fig. 145.—Black close-patterned (*mate*) *blonde* (Spanish style made at Bayeux).

mantilla is rapidly being supplanted by the modern bonnet and hat. Barcelona and Bayeux are the two principal centres for the manufacture of mantillas; and one may hope that the Spaniards will not allow this local and characteristic head ornament to fall out of use and disappear.

All the laces we have mentioned are made in lengths or bands upon pillows or cushions; ornament and meshed grounds being worked together.

We are now, however, going to notice those laces which are made in small pieces to be afterwards joined together; that is, by separate flowers and bits of ornament, or in segments analogous to those used in the needlepoint lace process. This manner of dividing a pattern for the pillow-lace method of work is certainly due to Belgian initiative.

Fig. 146. — Pillow-lace flower for *applique* lace (Flemish).

Guipures de Flandres (Flemish Guipures).—The first time that a Flemish lace-maker made a single flower with her bobbins upon a flat cushion (fig. 146), it probably did not occur to her that, by so doing, she had rendered her country a great service. Still, it is perfectly obvious that this peculiar modification in the making of pillow lace has, to a large extent, affected the industry.

A separate flower or ornament once completed, the ground, or some such means of connecting it with other similar flowers, was necessary. At first these connections were small bars of three or four threads plaited together. These bars would sometimes be enriched with little loops (*picots*). Separate ornaments and

Fig. 147.—Linen and white thread Flemish *guipure* curtain.

flowers with intervening looped bars or tyes (*bar-rettes picotées*), are the main features of *Guipure de Flandres*, a class of lace much in demand during the seventeenth century. Fine trimmings for albs and such-like were made in it ; and although its texture is flat and without reliefs, it derives a richness of effect from the ample and soft folds into which it falls. Bruges was specially noted for making this class of lace.

For furniture purposes Flemish *guipures* have been considerably used, in respect of hangings and trimmings about beds, toilet tables, and such-like (figs. 147 and 149).

Honiton Lace (fig. 146).—But they have also been used for ladies' costume. In Devonshire, Honiton has created and maintained a reputation for making pillow-lace *guipures* in the same manner as Bruges at an earlier date. But there is a marked

Fig. 148.—Pillow-made lace, *Duchesse guipure* (of Belgian make).

difference of style in pattern between the·Bruges and the Honiton laces.*

Duchesse Lace.—In Belgium, the lighter sorts of *guipures* are called *Guipure Duchesse* (see fig. 148).

* Besides the guipure laces, Honiton and other villages in Devonshire occasionally produce laces with a ground of regular meshes. Latterly some superior specimens have been made, in which this meshed ground is of needlepoint work. On the whole, however,

Application d'Angleterre (English Appliqué lace).—
As grounds of small meshes came into fashion, bars

Fig. 149.—Flemish *guipure* for furniture purposes.

and tyes in Flemish *guipures* disappeared, and lengths

Honiton lace has conserved its *guipure* character.   At the same time,
there is no reason why it should not make new departures and
achieve as high a success with these as with the styles of former
days, for which there is comparatively little present demand.

of meshed grounds (*réseaux*) were made, to which were applied the flowers or ornaments brought by other workers. This led to a more or less well-recognized division of labour. Certain workers excelled in making meshed grounds, and were solely employed in doing so; whilst others were restricted to the making of the flowers or ornament.

The new *appliqué* lace was in high favour during Louis XV.'s reign. The *vrai réseau* was the name given to the finest and softest of the mesh grounds made on the cushion. It was produced chiefly at Brussels. The mesh is hexagonal in shape, and its two longest sides consist of four plaits of four threads, the other four shorter sides being of two threads twisted twice. The delicate linen thread with which *vrai réseau* was produced possessed a fair creamy tone admirably suited to the complexions of blonde beauties, and this subtle charm of the lace gave rise to the custom of steeping other whiter laces in tea, so that they, too, might have the same kind of tint.

Appliqué lace was made in less quantities in England than in Belgium, notwithstanding that for purposes of trade it was always called English application (*Application d'Angleterre*) (fig. 150). Certain connoisseurs, anxious to show that they could not be imposed upon, adopted for this lace the Duc de Penthièvre's appellation : " *d'Angleterre de Flandres* ;" but this hybrid name never became general, and it was eventually deemed correct to speak of the lace as " *point d'Angleterre.*"

Of this we have evidence in a letter of the Duc de Luynes written in 1638 :—

" To-day were brought to Madame de Luynes the

laces she had chosen for the Queen, which, after use, revert to the ladies of honour. They consist of coverlets trimmed with *point d'Angleterre* for the big bed, and of pillow-cases similarly trimmed. This set of things cost thirty thousand livres, Madame de Luynes not deeming it necessary to give orders as to renewing the best coverlets belonging to the Queen." This extract shows that it was the custom for the bed trimmings of the Queen, upon their renewal each year, to pass into the possession of Her Majesty's ladies-of-honour. In spending no more than thirty thousand livres, Madame de

Fig. 150.—Application lace, called *Angleterre*, on pillow-made mesh ground.

Luynes is to be credited with the exercise of an economy and discretion not displayed by her predecessors in office.

Other decorations of a room would match those of the bed. The luxury displayed by Louis XV. in this direction is historic. The Duchesse de Bourbon has "a toilet table and her *bonhomme*" completely draped with spotted muslin and lengths of a beautiful "*dentelle a'Angleterre.*" *Monseigneur* the Dauphin had six comb cases and a dozen pincushions trimmed with "*Angleterre.*"

And we may finally quote the Princesse de Condé who had "two bathing cloaks trimmed with lace, and drapery about her bath edged with wide *Angleterre.*" It would be difficult to further extend the employment, not to say the abuse, of laces!

The patterns for these *appliqués* laces are generally insignificant in design, consisting for the most part of a few sprays or leaves, etc., scattered over a ground of meshes; this is obviously insufficient to give such lace artistic character. It will be well then to beware of the unstinted admiration so freely given, as a rule, to every old bit of *vrai réseau appliqué* lace which may come under notice. It is preferable to reserve one's appreciation for works in which good execution has been applied to graceful and well-composed designs.

In certain of the *appliqués* laces we meet with admirable contrasts of two sizes of meshes for the grounds, a device for obtaining variety in effect which had been happily used in the Argentan needlepoint laces.

The little town of Binche in Belgium has given its name to some pretty laces in which contrasting mesh grounds are used, as well as others in which the irregular barring of *guipures* is interchanged with regular mesh grounds (*réseaux*),—all with excellent result, especially as settings to patterns.

Application de Bruxelles.—About 1830 the invention

of machines for making fine nets (*tulle*) gave a new impulse to this class of work. Its costliness being considerably diminished through the substitution of *tulle* for the hand-made mesh ground or *vrai réseau*, a large trade has ensued in quantities of these Brussels application laces (*Applications de Bruxelles*), a name usually restricted to applications of lace, ornament, flowers, etc., upon Brussels *tulle* (fig. 151).

Fig. 151.—Flounce of Brussels application lace.

This simplification of process and lowering of price in its productions has been attended with some advantages. Larger pieces, for instance, such as big shawls and ample bridal veils, which, on the score of cost, could but rarely have been attempted with the hand-made net (*réseau*), are now easily made. It cannot be maintained, however, that machine-made *tulle* is as charming a material as *vrai réseau*; its dressing, as a rule, tends to make it wiry and harsh to the touch, and although this may be lessened by modification, the cotton thread, employed both for the lace ornaments and the *tulle*, lacks that delicate suppleness which is characteristic of the pure and fine flax thread used in *vraie Angleterre* laces. It is a matter even of congratulation when these modern cotton fabrics are not powdered with white lead, a pernicious and perfectly useless ingredient, frequently used, with dire effect to the health of the lace-workers and the good preservation of the lace.

Lace ornaments applied to *tulle* are not solely made on the pillow, some are of needlepoint work done in the same way as in the eighteenth century, when lace applications of pillow-made and needlepoint were sewn with admirable effects upon *vrai réseau*. Specimens of modern work, in which this mixture of lace applications occur, are given in figs. 152 and 153. Considerable skill is displayed in the little fillings or devices, *à jours* (see also fig. 110). The selection of details which are to be of needlepoint or pillow work rests with the designer of the pattern.

The town of Brussels, and one or two others, like Ghent and Alost, have derived handsome profits from this particular branch of the lace industry. Belgium has kept a pre-eminent position in it, notwithstanding efforts to compete with her on the part of England and France.

Tulle et Marli.—The fashion for meshed grounds (*réseaux*), so freely referred to in the course of our remarks upon pillow-made laces during the eighteenth century, culminated in the reign of Louis XVI. in one for almost patternless laces of mesh grounds with an insignificant little edging of loops. There were two kinds of such laces, distinguishable one from the other merely by the shape of the mesh; the one was called *tulle*, the other *marli*.

Although the precise date of its production cannot be stated, *tulle* would seem to have derived its fame

Fig. 152.—Lappet of Modern Brussels mixed needlepoint
and pillow lace.

as a fabric when made in the town bearing its name. Tulle, the chief town of Corrèze, is not far distant from Aurillac ; the character of its lace being simple, it was speedily imitated by many other places, but nowadays lace-making has disappeared from the province of Corrèze. But in an annual of 1775 there is mention of lace-makers at Tulle, certain Mesdemoiselles Gantes, aunts of the Abbé Gantes, who succeeded M. de Talleyrand as Bishop of Autun, and met his death at the guillotine after having been president of the constituent Assembly.

Lace was certainly manufactured at Tulle in the eighteenth century, and by some fortuitous circumstance the name of the town came to be given to all simple net grounds (*réseaux*) produced by the machine. Of these a considerable variety has been manufactured with sufficient

Fig. 153.—Bit of Modern Brussels application lace, with the roses worked in needlepoint.

differences to entitle each sort to be called by some qualifying title, such as Brussels *tulle*, Mechlin *tulle*, bobbin *tulle*, *tulle illusion*, *tulle point d'esprit*, etc. Originally, however, *tulle* was merely a lace of simple and regular meshes, almost bereft of ornament, and was called *tulle a fil* (thread net).

Marli lace no doubt takes its name from the village between Versailles and St. Germain, where Louis XIV. built his celebrated residence. The peculiarity of this lace consisted of its innumerable little square spots dotted over the gauzy *tulle*, which was frequently further embellished with light embroidery. It was used for *ruches* and cloud-like, vaporous coverings. The patterns of Tulle and Marli lace, whenever there were any, were composed of different little dots, little peas, or rosettes, but more often of little spots called *point d'esprit.*

Tulle and Marli lace was much worn by Marie Antoinette during the latter years of her life; entries of them occur over and over again with those for *blondes* and embroidered linens in Madame Eloffe's accounts with the Queen. Taste grew poorer and poorer, so far as ornamental lace was concerned, and when one meets with typical items like " a gauze fichu trimmed with white *pretention*," it is not difficult to realize that the art of lace as previously known, had become extinct. Moreover, this period was one of general sadness; the Queen wore black net laces only, and on leaving Versailles (October 6th, 1789) for the last time she distributed amongst her suite all that remained of her fans and laces.

Still, so great had been the demand for *tulle* a few years prior to the Revolution, that, according to the *Tableau de Paris* of that date, at least 100,000 work-women were engaged in France in its manufacture.

Many ladies applied themselves to making the simple mesh laces, for which comparatively few bobbins had to be used. Jean Jacques Rousseau recommended it as a suitable occupation for females :—

" But what Sophie knows best, and has been more thoroughly trained to, is work special to her sex, such as cutting out and making up her dresses. There is no needlework in which she is not an adept, knowing how to do it well, and doing it with pleasure; but that which she prefers above others is lace-making, because it necessitates a pretty attitude, and provides an exercise for the fingers which involves more grace and lightness of touch." (*Emile*, Book IV.).

The reference to a species of network at which Teresa Panza was able to make "eight *maravédis* a day," as she writes to her husband Sancho, is obviously not of the same nature as the fine bobbin *tulle* of which we have been speaking. Such delicate fabrics were virtually unknown during Cervantes' lifetime.

We cannot here undertake to speak of all the countries which have been, and are still, engaged in the pillow-lace industry. The principal types of pillow lace have, however, we hope, been so described as to at least enable our readers to identify their make when met with.

Every lace-making village or centre doubtless has some feature special to its work, but considerations of space prevent us from attempting a close survey of what at best are but minute variations in typical methods of manufacture.

The groundworks of certain German pillow laces consist of vermiculated plaitings. Russian laces are noted for patterns of meanders and sinuous forms (fig. 154). The Danubian provinces of Austria and Hungary make laces very similar in character of pattern.

Much as these laces at first sight may appear to be of distinctive manufacture, they will, upon examination, be found to come within the classification of *passements* for which the Auvergne is noted. The same methods of plying the bobbins and of producing tissue in strips, or bands, obtain in all these laces. So true is this, that Russian designs are frequently reproduced in laces made at Le Puy and Mirecourt.

Spain and Portugal enjoy a certain reputation for imitation white Chantilly laces. The island of Madeira, and places along the South American coast, have adopted traditions of the industry from Portuguese and Spaniards.

Pillow laces made by women in Ceylon and Travancore, as well as elsewhere in India, seem to owe more

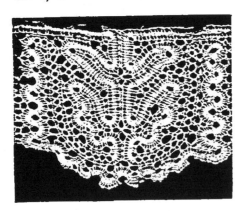

Fig. 154.—Russian pillow lace.

to the instruction of Portuguese than to that of either Dutch or English. And the specimens of Indian pillow laces, wrought with white and black threads, in the India Museum are apparently made in single pieces, and not, as in Honiton laces, by separate flowers, which are subsequently placed together for the ground to be worked in between them.

On the other hand, the Honiton method is known at Yokohama, where the Japanese Government has encouraged the development of a school of pillow-lace makers under the supervision of an English lady.

All pillow laces, from one end of the world to the other, are in a manner closely related one to another, though not to such an extent as to obscure certain slight peculiarities which contribute towards establishing characteristics of individuality. Circumstances of manufacture, together with local traditions, leave a trace upon the productions. Valenciennes lace, for instance, is made along the whole of the Franco-Belgian frontier. And yet each village or town between Bailleul and Ypres, and Ypres and Courtrai, etc., has its particular make, which is quite perceptible to any one on the look-out for it. It is the same in Normandy in respect of difference in manufacture between similar laces that may have emanated from Caen or Bayeux, notwithstanding the proximity of these two towns. The same remark applies to other lace centres near to one another.*

Members of conventual communities, sent by their superiors from one country or district into another, have introduced the art of lace-making into a locality where it was previously unpractised. Hence, Bayeux owes the establishment of its lace industry to nuns from the Convent *de la Providence* at Rouen. They were sent there at the end of the seventeenth century, to undertake the supervision of the workroom founded by the Canon Baucher in the old church of St. Georges. In 1747 the Abbé Suhard de Loucelles provided additional room for them in a house in the *Faubourg St. Loup*, close by the church of *Notre Dame de la Poterie*. In a short time more than four hundred young women were employed at the two sets of workrooms; and in 1758 the aldermen of the town presented to the *Intendant* of the province a pair of thread lace cuffs, which, according to the accounts of the municipality, cost 144 livres.

Dieppe and Cherbourg are also indebted, as are

* See observations as to this in Felix Aubry's Report of 1851.

many other places in Normandy, to nuns for their
lace industry.

The Revolution was as disastrous to pillow as to
needlepoint lace-making. Valenciennes never re-
covered from the effects of it; and Chantilly gradually
declined. At the Industrial Exhibition of Paris held in
1802, two Chantilly makers shared the honours, then
conferred, with several lace-makers from Le Puy; but this
was the last occasion when Chantilly asserted herself as
a lace-making town. She was superseded by Bayeux
and Caen, where intelligent direction struck out a new
line for the Chantilly make of lace, and gave new life
to it. In 1823, Madame Carpentier of Bayeux won
the first gold medal ever awarded for lace, and at each
succeeding exhibition Norman lace-makers have added
to their laurels. It may be safely said that France has
preserved an eminent place in the first rank of lace-
making countries.

Imitation Laces.—But the prosperity attaching to this
position has been seriously menaced through the invention of machines for making lace, more so as
regards pillow than needlepoint laces.

At Nottingham, whose reputation for its hosiery is
of long standing, the mechanical manufacture of bobbin
net or *tulle* was started in 1768. This was due to the
ingenuity of a workman named Hammond, who con-
ceived the idea of mechanically making a net tissue on
a stocking-knitting machine. Hammond's somewhat
crude machine was greatly improved upon in 1809 by
Heathcote's bobbin net-loom, since which time the
manufacture has flourished to a very important
extent.

Notwithstanding war and difficult commercial relations between England and France, a few English bobbin net-looms or frames were imported during the first Empire and set up in Lyons; and in 1817 a manufactory supplied with English plant was started at St. Pierre-lès-Calais.

The production of net in wide lengths being thus brought within the range of mechanical means, imitations of lace were made by hand embroidery upon machine-made net. In 1837 Jacquard invented his apparatus for fancy weaving, and an adaptation of it to the net-weaving machines gave rise to the production of *tulles brochés*, or flowered nets, which were still closer imitations of hand-made lace. The new manufacture, with its low-price results, speedily developed itself, and became a source of exceptional prosperity to the manufacturers engaged in it at Nottingham, Lyons, and St. Pierre-lès-Calais. In a few years St. Pierre, which had been but a small suburb of Calais with 1,000 or 1,200 inhabitants, grew into an important centre of manufacture with a population of from 35,000 to 40,000 persons.

Without lamenting over the progress which has taken place in the employment of machinery, and of which this century is so justly proud, we need not, therefore, hold with those who believe that machinery will supplant the hand.

It would be an obvious loss to art should the making of lace by hand become extinct, for machinery, as skilfully devised as possible, cannot do what the hand does. No doubt, from pretty patterns specially selected for reproduction by the machine, admirable illusions are produced to the satisfaction of those who have no care beyond superficial appearances. But these are the results of processes, not the creations of artistic handicraft. Where truth is wanting, art is absent— absent where formal calculation pretends to supersede emotion—absent, moreover, where no trace can be detected of intelligence guiding handicraft, whose hesitancies even possess peculiar charm. The machine truly supplies cheap substitutes ; but, as M. Didron well expresses it, " cheapness is never commendable in respect of things which are not absolute necessities ; it lowers artistic standard. Lace must inevitably lose the best features of its delight for us, on the day that it ceases to be precious and relatively rare." *

CONCLUSION.

THIS century has produced much lace, fashion being favourable to it. Never, probably, has so much been made as within late years, when 300,000 Frenchwomen alone have derived a livelihood from an industry which is one of the best alternatives to agricultural labour. It can be taken up, without damage to the work, at intervals between occupations in the fields. The implements and material, whether for making needlepoint or pillow lace, require little room, and can be stowed away with facility in the humblest of dwellings. The mother works her lace surrounded by her girls, who from their earliest years become instructed in the art. Jules Simon, in his book *L'Ouvrière,* and all economists interested

---

* Didron, *Report on the Decorative Arts at the Universal Exhibition of* 1878, p. 190.

in women's industries, have remarked how consonant the occupations of embroidery and lace-making are with family life.

We shall be glad if this, our book, in any way contributes towards maintaining the supremacy of lace-making by hand. Our remarks are intended to supply young women with information concerning women's artistic work, and it may perhaps be found useful by others who have an interest in such questions. All possibly may find in it some means for appreciating the difference between styles and periods of lace-making.

It will be seen that discrimination is necessary to a perception of the really admirable in ancient laces, and that unreflective enthusiasms vented upon old laces, merely because they are old, are in no way evidences of knowledge of and feeling for beauty of design and fine quality of workmanship. Our readers will be wary of being deceived by specimens of detached and incongruous bits of lace speciously and tastelessly made up by dealers.

Whilst, as regards modern lace, the fitness of its use, its special appositeness to certain portions of costume, and the qualities it should possess to be truly beautiful, will reveal themselves through study of the subject. This, too, will enlarge our sympathies with the humble and skilful workwomen who eke out a meagre living with their needles and bobbins.

A favouring return of general appreciation for hand-made lace and embroidery is observable in the interest with which books on the subject, by artists and *savants*, are read nowadays. Lace bibliography is becoming very considerable, and is supplemented with the highest advantage by museums of specimens for public inspection, and technical schools for the practice of the handicrafts.

Under such circumstances it would seem that these branches of contemporary art acquire sufficient vitality for a long and successful career in the future. Machines will respond to demands for large supplies; connoisseurs, however, will rely upon artistic handwork for what they want.

Women assuredly have at heart the interests of those artistic productions which come under the title of *Embroidery and Lace*. Young women who learn to draw and to paint, this book has been written for you above all others ; take your needles, cross your bobbins, and teach yourselves how best your designs may be put into execution ! Study the works of old time, and understand the possibilities of your art ! Our aim has been to help you in this direction, and, like the old authors, to have been of service "to virtuous women and other gentle spirits who feel the want of such arts " as embroidery and lace-making.

LIST OF LACES

ACCORDING TO THEIR NAMES AND LOCAL ORIGINS.

Printed by Hazell, Watson, & Viney, Ld., London and Aylesbury.

BIBLIOLIFE

Old Books Deserve a New Life
www.bibliolife.com

Did you know that you can get most of our titles in our trademark **EasyScript**™ print format? **EasyScript**™ provides readers with a larger than average typeface, for a reading experience that's easier on the eyes.

Did you know that we have an ever-growing collection of books in many languages?

Order online:
www.bibliolife.com/store

Or to exclusively browse our **EasyScript**™ collection:
www.bibliogrande.com

At BiblioLife, we aim to make knowledge more accessible by making thousands of titles available to you – quickly and affordably.

Contact us:
BiblioLife
PO Box 21206
Charleston, SC 29413

Printed in Great Britain by
Amazon.co.uk, Ltd.,
Marston Gate.